T0128715

CATACLYSM

Nick Gass

Cataclysm

A Scientific Basis for Some Old Legends

Why Genesis? Why Utnapishtim's Flood?
Why Noah? Why Eden? Why Kush?
Why the Confusion of Tongues?
Why Atlantis?
Why Mecca?
WHY US?

iUniverse, Inc.
Bloomington

Cataclysm
A Scientific Basis for Some Old Legends

iUniverse books may be ordered through booksellers or by contacting:

iUniverse
1663 Liberty Drive
Bloomington, IN 47403
www.iuniverse.com
1-800-Authors (1-800-288-4677)

ISBN: 978-1-4759-6537-7 (sc)
ISBN: 978-1-4759-6539-1 (e)
ISBN: 978-1-4759-6538-4 (hc)

Library of Congress Control Number: 2012922823

Printed in the United States of America

iUniverse rev. date: 03/18/2013

In Loving
Memory of
My Darling
Jean

"Stand by your Man"
"You are the Wind Beneath my Wings"

ILLUSTRATIONS

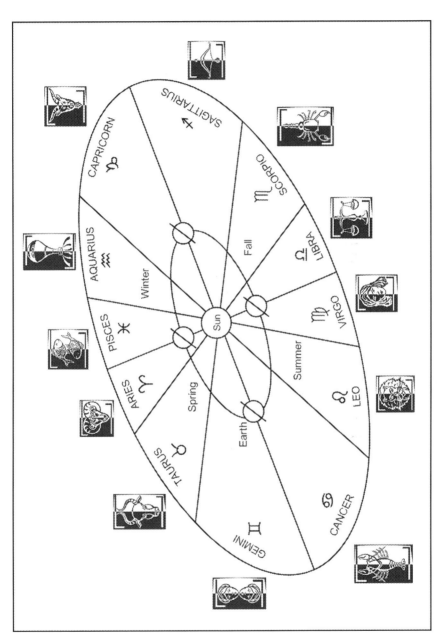

The Ancient Zodiac

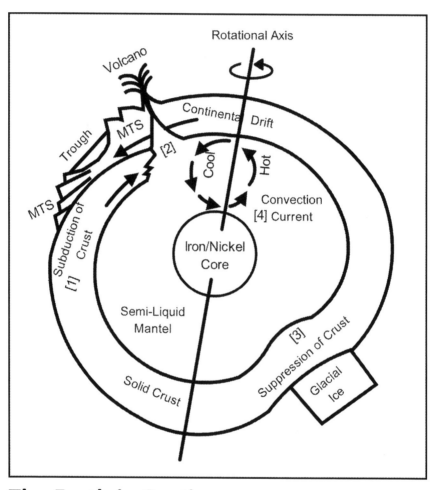

The Earth in Section

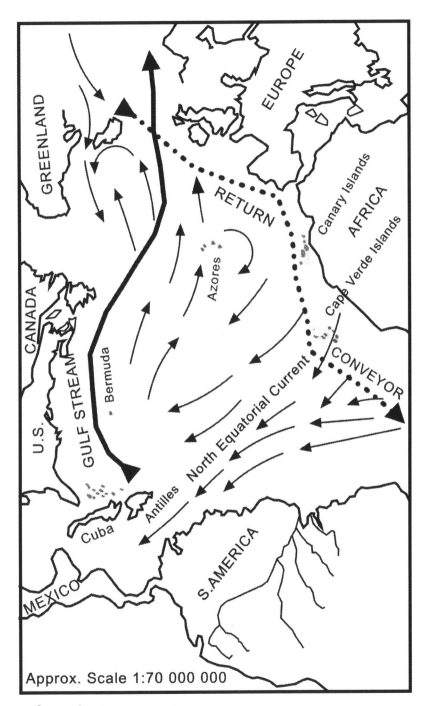

Atlantic Currents

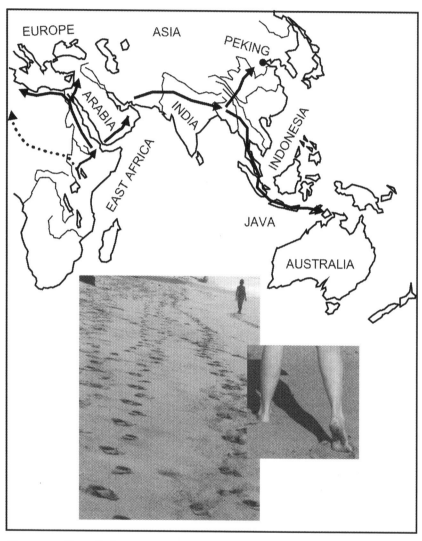

Out of Africa

Super Continent of Pangea

Map of the Middle East

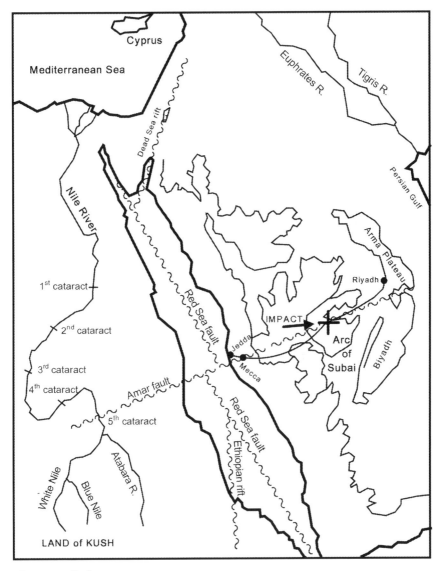

Astroblem

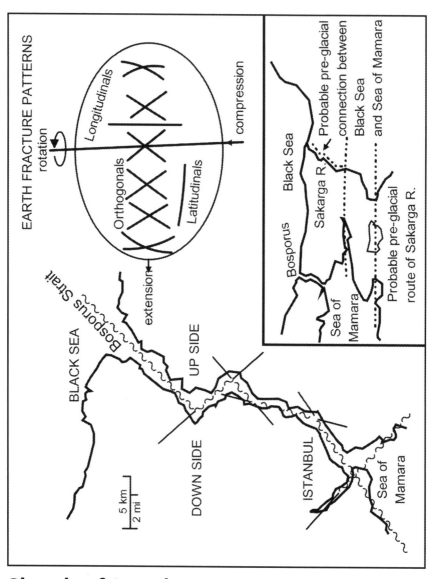

Sketch of Bosphorus Strait

Latitudinal Fracture Forming Cliff Face

Raised Beaches
(COURTESY OF GEOLOGICAL SURVEY of Newfoundland)

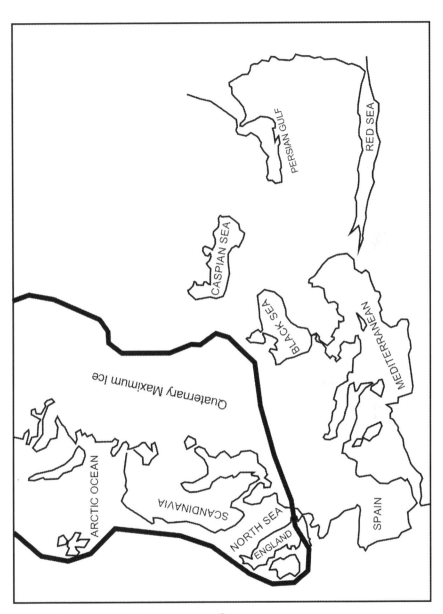

Maximum Extent of Ice

Salt Weathering

Persons Turned to Stone

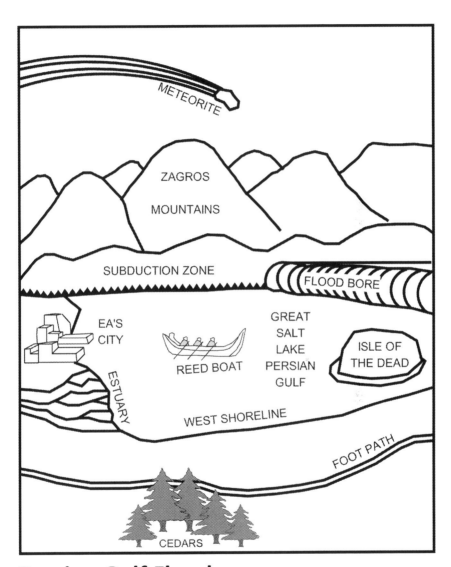

Persian Gulf Flood

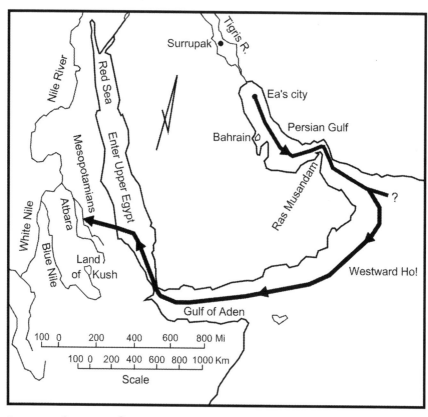

Invasion of Upper Egypt

ACKNOWLEDGEMENTS

I wish to sincerely thank the following people for their contributions and to acknowledge that without their help and encouragement there would be no book:

Marion Voth, who acted as secretary typist, agent, and general coordinator of the whole project;

My darling daughter Barbara, who typed the initial manuscript and saw the whole show on the road;

Charles Jeffrey, whose masterful illustrations, give the whole exercise such a visual component;

Judith Stableford, Alan Crozier, and Glen Patterson; all of whom proofread and offered constructive criticism throughout the process;

Kent Wallace, for photo of salt weathering;

Earle Brown, for the gift of *The Gilgamesh*; and

Ron Voth, for the photography of the author.

CONTENTS

PREFACE

MOST PEOPLE DON'T READ the preface, but you can hardly afford not to if you wish to get your money's worth out of such a short book.

So why yet another tract on the Middle East, and why do I think that I'm the one to write it? Plato's tale of Atlantis, which he picked up down in Egypt, has been hyped up to such an extent that no one is very interested anymore. That's a real shame because there are some very interesting elements to the whole story. Gavin Menzie's new book *The Lost Empire of Atlantis*[1] does a great job with the tale. It doesn't stand alone, and the connections to other legends of the area are what provide the renewed interest that I will attempt to illustrate.

So why me? Well, I am reliably advised that readers wish to know "Who is this guy?" so they can judge the probability of authenticity for themselves. That sounds like pretty good advice, so I'll attempt to provide my believable background and thereby my assumed authority to tell the tale. Next, "they" tell me that readers will wish to know why I ever presumed to write the book in the first place. They opine that it won't cut it to say that it's just because that's the sort of thing that I would do. Therefore, I am going to have to be a bit more up front and specific. My take on the whole thing is that there is a lot more involved in these old legends than a high tide in an old city. But the main question at this point is "Who am I to presume to set the record straight?" Perhaps because the actual historic

1 Menzies, Gavin *The Lost Empire of Atlantis*. (New York: William Morrow Publishers, 2011).

record is so sketchy and fragmented, various authors have filled in the missing pieces with heroic inventions of their own. Readers are majorly sceptical. Well, you be the judge.

First of all, an admission: I've never been there. However, a number of my friends in the oil business have, and their tales have left me with a high level of interest in whatever happened in those early days of eschewing the hunter-gatherer format to settle down to an agricultural future in the Middle East, or what were Eve's thoughts on the matter? Didn't she sort of pine for the good old hunter-gatherer days? Not to be, Eve dear! The point I'm trying to make is that Atlantis was only one event among many on mankind's journey to intellectual sovereignty, and since Menzies [1] has done such a great job, I will not bother with it.

For a long time I had been a somewhat rambunctious field geologist, but my peripheral eyesight began to fail, which make it difficult for one to go "bushwhacking." So the next best thing is to write about it, but who is going to read that boring stuff?

However, I was also a fairly respectable cartographer (mapmaker) and had a long-standing interest in ancient legends. So there's a connection. Do you recall the Greek legend of Jason and the Golden Fleece? Well, they were a bunch of prospectors up around the Black Sea. A "fleece" is still the preferred method for capturing the fine alluvial gold. So you see, as distant as that legend may be, there is still a connection through the area, the descriptions and the topography if nothing else.

But there is something else that should be cleared up before proceeding. Many people don't have a very clear idea of the difference between myth and legend and use the two interchangeably to the denigration of both. We should probably define how the two concepts are to be regarded for this work.

It is probably true that both myth and legend have been largely dismissed as "fairy stories," but that is a major oversight to my mind. We won't deal with myths in this work, as legend is to be our focus, whether they are from the Bible or some other narrative, we will attempt to salvage the core truth in order to incorporate the basic message into our view of history, because legends play a very useful role in directing our efforts as to "where to dig."

A legend is taken to be a true story, embellished and distorted with the telling as the blanks are filled in as befit each storyteller and the tenor of the times. Only the core tale survives a variety of political and cultural mores. The "spin" changes occasionally, but the essential historic validity of the story remains largely intact. Not that different from what we are treated to daily by the media today.

A myth is a much different concept from a legend and serves a much different purpose. Myths are fanciful explanations for what the subconscious recognizes as something that we should perhaps believe, or at least pay attention to, perhaps in the realm of the collective unconscious. One really needs to read Joseph Campbell for a more definitive description. Myths appear to be an affirmation of what an intuitive person instinctively knows, depending on the individual, although it is often majorly skewed. Myths are generally non-historic in the sense of time but are more psychological in the sense of human nature (i.e., they are timeless).

Wishing to expand my understanding of the ancient Middle East, I read the book *Legend*[2] by David Rohl, a British Egyptologist. That provided a fascinating factual background for many of the Middle Eastern legends. Then a couple of oceanographers from Woods Hole, Massachusetts, wrote a book called *Noah's Flood*[3], which was again an absorbing read. But they didn't explain why it happened. Well, that would be a pretty straightforward task for me.

So why does this prairie-cum-mountain geologist presume to present an explanation for Noah's Flood? Sounds a little farfetched! Well, you see, I wasn't always a prairie rose. My origins go back to the East Coast, and my oceanic technical skill obtained from having been a fisherman who attempted to ride out a hurricane in an open boat. If this has made a permanent impression on you, it gets weirder than that, so I should perhaps fill in some of the blanks. There is always some sort of connective thread.

Let's start with the legend of me. My 6' 2" dad went off to war in 1939 and left six-year-old me to be "the man of the house."

---

2 Rohl, David, *Legend: The Genesis of Civilization*, (Mississauga: Random House, 2000).
3 Ryan and Pitman, *Noah's Flood*. (Toronto: Simon and Schuster, 2000).

That's where I gained my reverence for women, courtesy of a darling mother and three sweetheart sisters.

Regardless of the audacity of the picture that whole scenario may invoke, my young brain, being the man of the family, took it to heart, and I matured very rapidly into the responsible male who looked after "his women." Except just the opposite was true and they spoiled me rotten. I learned quickly, and I soon had my own boat and 'riggin' to advance the family fortune when I was twelve years old. I could go 'fishin' and had more money than any of the other kids in this poor lumbering community. Actually, the fishing was pretty lucrative, and I envisioned myself in an entrepreneurial capacity of the "fish for rum" trade with the Caribbean. But it was not to be. The Independent Order of the Daughters of the Empire (IODE) plucked me out of high school and sent me to Dalhousie University where I enrolled in math, chemistry, and physics—pretty standard stuff in those days and pretty boring. Then, in fourth year, I needed another science to complete a degree. An engineering friend advised taking geology, as that was where all the pretty girls in science gravitated for their fourth science. It was love at first sight. I mean geology, not the girls. Well, perhaps some of the girls too—where did all those beauties come from? I hung in there until I got my master's degree. There were only two professors in the department.

The first was George Vibert Douglas, a Carnegie professor showered by this institution with all the latest equipment to the point where the chemistry and physics departments were jealous of us "rock knockers" and our sophisticated equipment. They even sent their prettiest graduate student down to partake of the cornucopia, but that's a story for another book (goodness, love doesn't exempt academics)!

The second professor was Dr. Nordeau Goodman. He was only half-time, but I think perhaps the only ever Rhodes Scholar in mineralogy. He was a great believer in the Oxford Method. He would take us out into the field with perhaps a case of beer or bottle of wine and introduce us to some of the most bizarre mineralogical occurrences on the planet, and we had to figure them out through discussion and argument. Did his methods work? Well, they sure did for me. When I ended up at an oil company in Alberta, I was frequently placed in some research project or other, a few of which I'll deny to this day. That got to be a little stressful, so I became a Sputnik Education Recruit. For younger readers who may not recognize that syndrome, when the Russians launched the first earth satellite, politicians blamed science education in the schools for the West being one-upped by the Soviets. There was a downturn in the economy, so many people in different fields of science saw it as their patriotic duty to vacate insecure industrial jobs and go into education. Despite the cop-out excuses, I loved teaching kids, and they quite liked me. But I kept my hand in the geological thing by incorporating a mineral exploration company, which I and my darling wife operated for thirty years. We never made much money, but we loved our way through the beautiful mountain summers.

When that all ended, I decided to apply my expertise to authenticating some of our more precious ancient legends. Jean would be proud of me! If there is one overarching thing that Dr. Goodman taught me, it was how to connect the dots.

I also must own up to another gift of the fates. When they were cleaning out the basement of an old school of mine, I spied an old British atlas over fifty years old. I don't really wish to disparage more modern editions (well, actually I do), but this older edition had everything but the inhabitants' names on it, even the location of the sand dunes. That old edition coupled with Google Earth's outlines was almost like being there. Indeed, taking some of the standard Canadian explanations for the earth's geological expressions and an avant-garde thesis of a pretty young Calgary geologist, I "was" there. I will yet tell you the central thesis, but just the other day I ran into a fellow author, and he said that he had actually been to one of my crucial "hang the whole thing on this peg" spots, and it is exactly as I said it would be. "*Mon ami*, Perault."

Of course, whenever I came up against those half-told tales in the Middle East, Dr. Goodman's voice would ring in my ears: "But what is that item you are considering connected to, and what effect would that have had on your conclusion?" He was the perfect template for taking on a problem as old as civilization itself. What a gift he was.

But all the foregoing is personal, sort of the baggage that I bring to the rail. What we really need is a more objective view. I can do that, as unconventional as my perspective may at first appear. It's really not that far afield; however, I have great difficulty with the hype that our darling legends have been subjected to, and I won't stand for it. If it's not rational, don't expect it from me, because I find hype a travesty of the human intellect. I'm not a mathematician, but I do have great respect for those guys. They tend to be rational.

Right away I detect some sort of invisible dividing line, which I presume is going to require some sort of definition. Fiction is perhaps the most pervasive genre of our modern age, but where is the dividing line between fact and fiction? We call our stuff theory. Well, what is that if it's not fiction with a few numbers attached? We need some potion to help define the boundaries, because scientific "reality" often starts out with conjured-up images.

The purpose of this book is not to grind one axe or the other but to tap into all sources in order to tell a fairly rational, logical, consistent story in a cogent manner. There has recently been a rash of science writing aimed at satisfying the perceived increased interest in science by the general public. Radio programs such as *Quirks and Quarks* and television documentaries too numerous to mention have pandered to the public appetite for a greater understanding of our world, our universe, and our place in it. Hopefully, we are consistent with the emerging grand tradition. The subjects are so immense that volumes could be written, but then few would care to read. Accordingly, choices have been made and judgments executed in order to include only what is deemed necessary in order to paint the picture. Much of the detail that might be seen as extremely interesting to scientists in the field has been left out. In short, the exformation vastly exceeds the information. Hopefully, the distillation will be of interest to the greatest possible number of readers. There has been little attempt to avoid controversy; in fact, perhaps just the opposite is true. The objective is a story that hangs together for most people. Controversy has a way of moving one to get busy and compile the necessary data to prove, or at least authenticate, a different point of view. By throwing down the gauntlet, the truth begins to sort itself out.

The ultimate aim of this work will be to cast a different light on the old legends through a multidisciplinary approach to all the evidence areas that might possibly bear on the subject. On the journey, raising awareness of our rich heritage should tell a good story. In the process, there will certainly be unanswered questions. Some tentative solutions may present themselves, but by and large, the objective is not to provide answers. It is an attempt to present a reasonable and sequential account of events as they may have occurred over a period of millions of years. The greatest success to be hoped for is that some reader might be in a position to affect a submarine exploration program and find this book a sufficient motivation to act on it. There are geologists out there who have 'made it' in economic terms, and we need them to get behind this idea of submarine exploration in and around the Mediterranean.

It's funny—or, rather, peculiar—how our modern world is built on mathematical concepts, yet we average citizens have such rudimentary understanding of those concepts, beyond perhaps calculating our kilometres per litre or picking six numbers for the lottery. However, the history of numbers is itself interesting. Yes, in our hunter-gather days, all it probably amounted to was one, few, or many. In fact, in the early days of the North American fur trade, we were partners with the first nations, until, in my opinion, we learned that they couldn't count. Then they became the victims of our commercial exploitation. But learning to count was one of the very early achievements of "civilization," because trade and taxes were civilization. Oh sure, the phases of the moon and the menstrual cycle gave numbers a celestial connection, but these were not nearly as important as bushels of einkorn or numbers of shell beads. We, normal persons, don't need numbers much beyond toting up the machushla at the end of the month. Numbers do have another life. Bishop Usher added up the lives of the prophets to determine the kick-start of when everything got going (6,000 years ago) for one thing. Then the rate of radioactive decay projects a somewhat more protracted period for the beginning of time. Many of our ancient scribes and purveyors of the oral traditions just ignored numbers altogether. Thus, we are often faced with attempting to fit the tale into the time available. Not that we can't do that, but of necessity, there is frequently a broad margin of error, time wise.

Numbers have been almost as slow coming into the general human consciousness as letters. But then, you have to admit that little squiggles on a page don't show much of a relationship to the numbers of people we celebrate killing in a war, or stars in the sky. But don't ask me to solve a quadratic equation or even tell you what it means. Yes, I know, we do have a sort of guarded reverence for that priestly class we call mathematicians, but then they do have an in with the gods that we don't share. Isn't that correct?

Much of the early concept of numbers, beyond simple record-keeping, grew out of the study of astronomy. Somehow or other early astronomers detected the precession of the earth as it appears to move against the patterns of stars in the sky. They attached great significance to this visual phenomenon, even though it actually means zip, because all spinning objects precess. Recall the slow arc that your child's spinning top moved through across the living room floor. Well, that's precession, and because the earth is spinning, the earth sort of does the same thing. The entire phenomenon has come down to us as the pseudo-science of astrology, from which numerology and a plethora of secret societies obtain. All good magical stuff, except that it has nothing to do with anything except recording the precessive movement of the globe (approximately one degree in a lifetime, or 30 degrees in 2,250 years). Each of the 12 "houses" of the zodiac subtends 30 degrees of arc, and we are now about to enter the Age of Aquarius (from the musical *Hair*). Don't expect much to change, except for what is described in the epilogue of this book, which has nothing to do with astrology. The one useful adjunct of the zodiac thingee is that it can be used to date artefacts of prehistory if the ancients make reference to the position of the stars, as they apparently do for the great pyramids of Egypt.

I have always found astrology to provide a good illustration of numbers vs. science, perhaps because it involves a lot of real stuff with numbers attached. So I will attempt to use this good fun artefact, to illustrate that "thin partitions do their bounds divide," as Shakespeare said.

Everything from extraterrestrials to autistic forbearers have been used to explain the origins of astrology, but the simple truth is that no one has the slightest idea. Actually, give astrology its due. It probably gave rise to a number base of twelve, although most people couldn't count beyond ten fingers and toes so that base won out, certainly an improvement over one, few, or many.

Are You a Scorpio or a Gemini?

Because "moderns" don't appear to put much stock in astrology, I should perhaps pause for a minute to explain a few of the essentials. As the earth orbits the sun in a year, you get to see every one of the twelve imaginary patterns of the zodiac that selected stars make against the dark night sky. Each of these patterns constitutes a "house" that subtends 30 degrees of arc. Depending on your birthday, you are said to have been born under a particular sign, which is the central star pattern for that time of year; this is alleged to invest you with certain character attributes. Dog breeders have long recognized that a "winter dog" (born in winter) tends to have a different disposition than a "summer dog," so there may actually be something to the ancient beliefs. However, psychology has supplanted much of astrology's primordial attempt to classify our demeanour and claims that your familial setting and genetics have much more to do with your disposition than your "stars" do. Psychologists don't tend to be the most romantic of our breed, so perhaps there may still be something else out there. But the patterns don't stay in one place in the sky forever, due to the slow precession of the earth in its orbit, once around every 27,000 years (rotation on our axis is once every twenty-four hours; revolution once around the sun every 365 ¼ days). So perhaps only five or six zodiacal houses have gone by since the glaciers melted and man began to settle down. I'm ignoring the speculation of what may have happened before that, but even so, the ancients were intrigued by the whole thing, and whenever they chance to mention it we can extrapolate a fairly accurate date.

For many years, the Roman emperors could attach additional days to their months, sort of willy-nilly in competition with other emperors, who professed to be gods themselves. Thus July (Julius Caesar's month) could have thirty-one days in competition with August (Augustus Caesar's month). But, blimey! No one wanted February, probably because it was cold and had that problem with groundhogs.

The Greeks had been much more attune to attending to their knitting and determined the square on the hypotenuse. Then the Arabs got really serious with their decimal system, and math was unceremoniously yanked out of the hands of the gods. Except for bragging about all the deer we had slain, there really wasn't much use for the number thing. Perhaps the whole item might have proceeded much faster if we had just left it to the girls—at least they could count to twenty-eight.

So, where is all of this number stuff heading? Well, with all the major personal concerns of death and dying, living a good life (or the "good" life) eternal life, just reward, and all that incalculable stuff, we have sort of left the number's game to charlatans, accountants, or scientists—not really the bread and butter of our daily lives. But then every little once in a while we get blindsided by the miracle of numbers and what they appear able to do for us. In 1997, a minor event occurred in the broad field of astronomy that received only passing public notice. This small technological breakthrough might eventually make more difference to how we view our place in the universe than all the more spectacular stuff put together. The technical term for the new procedure is nulling interferometry, and it involves math—big time. This is the technique of using out of phase light to blank out the direct light coming from a star. Once the bright starlight is nulled, the much weaker, polarized, reflected light from orbiting planets can be seen. Subsequently in the new century, an older technique of monitoring the dimming of starlight as a planet passes in front of it appears to be more effective, as the results from orbiting telescopes have improved. To date, some one thousand planets have been identified. Most are large gas giants, like our own Jupiter, but a handful are small, rocky orbs, like Earth, Mars, Venus, and Mercury. No matter how often we get hoisted on our own petard, there is one thing we humans seem to hold as a self-evident truth: seeing is believing. That is most likely why we will go to Mars instead of just trusting the exploration to much cheaper and more efficient robots, because they can't "see" like we can. However, it is no longer the idea of traversing a dead planet that fires the imagination. It is the prospect of contacting other intelligent life that drives us on. Amir Acycl, in his book, *Probability*

1: Why There Must Be Intelligent Life in the Universe,[4] says that the idea is not new. He quoted Epicurus from 300 BC. that there are many worlds that we don't yet know about, all of them having "living creatures and plants and other things we see in this world." Old Epicurus must have sounded to his contemporaries as if he was into the magic mushrooms, but here we are at the beginning of the third millennium AD with the old Greek's prophecy as a very real possibility. We may very well make contact within the lifetime of some of us living today. Then, what a dilemma it will be. What will we say to them? Well, what a story we have to tell of where we came from, how we got here, and what disasters befell us on the way. They will doubtless have their own tale of a climb to intellectual sovereignty, but although there may be some similarities, it will not be the same. It behoves us to know our own historic record in a lot more detail than most of us do at present. So, this book can act as a first hit rehearsal for our moment of glory.

After all, we do not want to be upstaged by a bunch of extraterrestrials. And a time scale into which we can fit events is a primary requirement—geologic time, evolutionary time, time before, time since—and even though we don't know the exact times, we have "pretty" good estimates with reasonable margins of error. Sorry, Bishop Usher, considerably more than six thousand years.

Some night when you can't sleep, turn on the radio and listen for a few minutes to the crackle of static. It is an awesome thought then to think that at least some of the radiation being picked up by your antennae is believed to be cosmic "stuff" coming from space that was left over from when it all began—the Big Bang. Cosmological physicists are forever writing learned papers about what may have been happening nanoseconds after ignition. Such proclivity for mathematical constructs is not of great interest to a very wide audience. Of somewhat greater appeal, the following ten billion years sees a universe of stars caught in the gravitational whirlpools we call galaxies, flying off in all directions at ever-increasing velocities. So what civilizations may have arisen in some far-off corner of the universe, figured it all out and expired in their

---

4 Aczel, Amir D, *Probability 1: Why there Must be Intelligent Life in the Universe.* (Orlando: Houghton Mifflin Harcourt, 1999).

own private Armageddon "unknelled, unhonoured, and unknown." Perhaps we don't care to dwell on such thoughts, as the déjà vu factor sends chills up the spine. Collectively, we seem to have an unconscious sense that, except for the immutable laws of quantum mechanics and thermodynamics and some peculiar quirks in the statistical probability of evolutionary processes, we might not even exist. "There but for the grace of God go I!"

Hopefully we have been able to set the stage for latter events. The tragedy was just one of many, some often initiated by the victims themselves. One might certainly appreciate a tearful God who decided to start all over again. It is not the celestial act itself which is so intriguing but the mechanism which follows a somewhat more comprehensible line than simple "belief." Oh sure, belief is involved, but the "how" is what I find intriguing. And back off, Cecil B. DeMille. We can explain God's expertise without resorting to fanciful fairy stories.

INTRODUCTION

IT IS COMFORTING TO come back from such high-minded contemplation of the cosmic in our lives to the old familiar neighbourhood. Some 5–10 billion years ago, in a perfectly ordinary spiral galaxy, our star began to rise—literally. Twentieth-century geologists and astronomers have filled in much of the detail of the early history of our solar system. But what is truly incredible is that someone else very far back in our own antiquity possessed pretty much the same information. The possible source can prove to be a very controversial subject, open to a great deal of personal opinion and broad speculation. A number of authors have drawn attention to the existence of this knowledge, but that doesn't appear to have had a whole lot of impact on our belief systems. It is probably worth repeating here in order to set the stage for the awesome journey on which we are about to embark. In case you don't have a copy of the book of Genesis from the Hebrew Old Testament (King James Version) handy, the required verses will be provided. This effort to supply supportive astronomical and geological reference should not be interpreted as any attempt to reinterpret the Bible. It is provided with a view to integrating some of the profound biblical references into a current geological/astronomical context. It should never be viewed as detracting from the inspirational narrative of the Good Book. Indeed, it should add a firm measure of wonder and awe to our perception of the insight and knowledge of our very distant forbearers. The method of explanation and clarification chosen has a very long history. The marginal notes of Jewish scholars in the

Talmud sometimes occupy more space than the original text. It is most unfortunate that our Christian traditions have not retained this very lively teaching device. However, I should not point fingers, as I don't use it very much either—I just wish that I had more courage.

One of the prime challenges for the task at hand is in the sequencing of biblical events. The actual text itself is quite straightforward, but the order in which they have been assembled leaves a lot to be desired. It is relatively certain that the earlier stories of the Bible were handed down from generation to generation via the oral tradition. This fact is substantiated by the knowledge that these stories go way back, to a time long before writing or any form of permanent type-recording had been invented. The very antiquity of the stories is something of a marvel in itself. The transmission of the historical knowledge was the preserve of the guslars. Their role was to keep the history intact while engaging the attention of the audience. Truly great storytellers feel fully justified in embellishing certain aspects or reordering particular sections in order to enhance the impact (not terribly different from advertising today). The scribes who first in scripted the stories would have unwittingly perpetuated any such alterations in addition to the usual errors of transcription. Much of the text of Genesis is believed by some scholars to have originated in languages other than Semitic. Then errors of translation would have compounded the problem all down the line. In addition, it would be naive to believe that the scribes were not under political pressure to massage the stories to make them appear consistent with the current conventional wisdom. Some of the recent translations are being accused of all or some of the above tribulations. The objective of these observations is to draw attention to the arena of ordinal (sequential) relationships as problematic and to suggest some restructuring in order to reflect what we presently know about the order of the actual events in earth history. In no way is the basic validity of the text ever questioned; au contraire, the intent is to reinforce the textual validity by soliciting support from other sources, namely geology, astronomy, and archaeology. It is with some trepidation and a great deal of humility that the task is undertaken. The format of the first chapter will be to present the biblical text, and then provide an explanatory comment consistent with what is known and what may be reasonably assumed. Then, because the biblical texts abandon us somewhere in the late Cretaceous, we will have to fill in much of the last 2.5 million years by relying on what we know, or think we know, of the effects of God's great glaciations as an instrument of change with the naked ape in the crosshairs. Then, or course, we must deal with the original motivation for such an undertaking as this. No, not just a lifetime of yearning to write script for Cecil B. Demille but a sincere desire to bring our pre-written history back into focus for us common folk.

We will need to invoke the biblical flood, which set the Hebrews on their long and tortuous path to the Promised Land. Their little stopover in Ur of the Chaldese will be used to cast a minimum of light on how an already existing flood story may have become mixed up with Noah's account. The greatest impact of the pre-existing tale is almost one to one correspondence with the geological evidence

But we really need to set the stage so that those of a non-religious orientation may come along as well. For this reason, we will take a cursory look at the Pleistocene glaciation and its role of sculpting that peculiar looking naked ape wandering around out on the savannas of Africa, his false starts and eventual emergence as God's primo creation with no trifling bit of pathos involved, how we may have achieved consciousness, emigrated, bleached out (some of us), and fallen into the cement mixer that was the Middle East. Then we will have to stand on a no-nonsense modern geological position in order to give incontestable evidence for how the flood (or floods) might have come about, only to discover that someone was there before us some eight thousand years ago (yeah). I don't know about you, but that kinda hurt—my expounding on all that great scientific intellectual property only to discover that someone had come to the same conclusion eight thousand years before and never paid any tuition at all.

In teaching, we used to have a half-believed syndrome that we called serendipity, which sort of meant that everything fell into place naturally. There was never such a thing as super serendipity or serendipity in spades. It does seem to me that something more than management alone provided me with one of geology's most recent "avant-garde" theories to explain Noah's Flood. Then to have been gifted a book with the ancient sentence from the Gilgamesh that just matter of factly describes the second flood! The gods are smiling—*ne c'est pas*?

CHAPTER 1:   MOSES SUPPOSES

FOLLOWING ALONG WITH THE general thesis that we practitioners of the oral tradition have practiced from time immemorial, the beginning comes later. I will present my version of some of the contents of the good book in a somewhat historical come geological/archaeological context, rather than a, b, c. Right up front, I should acknowledge my awe at how people way back then knew so much. There were, of course, no universities, no government research projects, and precious little astronomy, apart from "star gazing" (I think). But, just perhaps, there is something we may have missed, having depended so heavily on my compatriots of the ancient Hebrew spin. Of course, as with all oral traditions, it was crafted to suit the probable audience and lost (or gained) a bit when set down by scribes on clay tablets for all time. But some of the individual items and ideas are indeed awesome (inspired, if you will).

I know that persons of a religious persuasion say that it is all inspired. I have no argument with that. "How?" is my question. However, I will not even address that, as again there is no answer. I will only offer a few suggestions as to how a few of the items may have come to be included. The idea is not to provide historical fact, because no one actually knows, and simply "inspired" doesn't put enough meat on the bones. I would wish for the more tentative folk to believe that there probably are good rational reasons for the inclusion of some items and the exclusion of such a wide plethora of others. So I will just provide a sort of "jocular ride" of speculation to heighten interest and insert the query "if we only knew."

So let us start at the beginning, "a very good place to start." But hold on now. We have an argument as to what and where is the beginning! The choice appears to fall between Moses himself and his prophetic book. So let's go with the Man and his diatribe first, because we can conjure up lots of speculation there.

Most people have probably heard the romantic tale of the Egyptian princess finding the babe in the basket floating in the bulrushes. ("You found what? Where? How many times have I told you to stay away from those Goshen swamps!") There is quite a similar story from the Malobharata of India (c. Ray 1889) only in that one it was a god that impregnated the lady and probably considerably prior to the Moses story. Also Sargon 1 is alleged to have done his time in a basket over on the Tigris/Euphrates River before establishing the Akkadian Empire, and apparently some Hittite Queen launched a veritable flotilla of babes in baskets—just seems to have been the thing to do. Anyhow, Moses appears to have grown up and to have been a very honourable and perhaps somewhat sensitive man in the Egyptian court.

The Egyptian Book of the Dead is a document that itemizes the behaviour required in order to advance into their version of the Great Beyond. Chris Hedges, in *The World as It Is* (Page 10)[5] says that 5 of the Hebrew Ten Commandments are based on admonishments contained in the Book of the Dead. Certainly Moses would have been familiar with it.

Just a bit of a recap though before we launch into our own version of the story of Moses. Why are we doing this? Well, much of this book touches on areas of disbelief, so we will attempt to help our readers bridge that gap before we get too far afield. Ian Morris in *Why the West Rules—For Now* (Page 218)[6] implies that there was an era of great unrest around the Mediterranean due to a massive drought caused by global warming. Joseph had been sold into slavery in Egypt by his brothers but rose to be a grand visor of some sort, at least for the northern areas. So he brought his relatives down from Canaan to establish them on the fertile Delta land of Goshen,

---

5 Chris Hedges, *The World As It Is* (New York: Nation Books, 2011), 10.
6 Ian Morris, *Why the West Rules For Now* (Toronto: McClelland & Steward, 2011), 218.

where they did very well. But after Joseph's death, things kind of fell apart. The Egyptians apparently moved to drive the Hyksos (another group of Canaanites who were dominant in the Delta) out of the area. And the Israelites apparently became a subject race, making bricks and building stuff for the Egyptians. Moses, "on tour" of one of these venues, observes an overseer beating one of the slaves and kills him, making a felon of himself, so he has to flee somewhere out east across the Sinai, where he is taken in by one of Egypt's vassal administrators who is also a holy man of Yahweh. Then Moses marries his daughter and has a couple of kids. His wife seems to have persuaded him that there would be little hope for the little band of Jews unless they accepted Yahweh. Moses goes her one better he writes the Law and the Prophets—but we are getting way ahead of our story. Moses decides to go back to Egypt and persuade the Pharaoh to release the Israelites from bondage, but Pharaoh is having none of that, so Yahweh brings down ten plagues on Egypt. Pharaoh stands firm until the last one—the death of all Egyptian first born (Jewish Passover). Then Pharaoh relents and "lets my people go."

So what has Moses been doing with himself all of this time? Well, one might guess that he is spending much of his days back with his old professors compiling the book of Genesis. And this is where the pace quickens, because the first twenty-five verses comprise a compendium of geological items.

After our little spiel in the prologue about going back to the beginning of time, it might strike some as peculiar that we would start off the main tract with the story of Moses, which is relatively recent. The question is not so much where did Moses get all this scientific stuff—that seems relatively obvious: his old professors— but where in tarnation did they get it? So the intent is to sort of set the stage using Moses to underscore the concept that there was a whole bunch of pretty accurate information out there more than three thousand years ago, and if Moses' profs had it, then others had it too. Probably just as today. If some cataclysm were visited on the earth, it would not be useful information that would survive, but the hype surrounding those who are front and centre politically. The story of Moses is admirably suited to tell 'our' story, as well as to create wonder about what else. The political and religious components of our background have dominated for far too long. There is other stuff out there that is just as important for our understanding. And I'll try to help out, because with some reservations that appears to be my role—Yahweh willing.

After Pharaoh released the Israelites, he seems to have said to himself, "What am I doing? I won't have any cheap labour." So he gave chase and caught up with the exodus at the Reed Sea, not the Red Sea as previously texted. Apparently, there has been a missed translation from the Greek. The Red Sea is a bit farther along. Anyway, the Israelites disappear into the reeds and the heavy Egyptian chariots and armour get stuck in the mud. But one might imagine that the whole scenario frightened the daylights out of our domestic bricklayers and Moses's precious tablets got dumped. When several volunteers came back to retrieve the tablets the next day, they got some of them mixed up and in the wrong order (the Arabic numbering system wasn't due for a thousand years). As you can see, the story as it has comes down to us through the ages, requires a deft hand to put them back in the same order that Moses inscribed them.

Isbouts[7] presents a somewhat different scenario with regard to subsequent events of the Exodus than in the past. We know that Moses did not go directly "home" to Canaan, first of all because he didn't know where it was; he was an Egyptian and his followers had never been there either. In addition, the Egyptians kept up a steady power demo over through the vassal buffer states, and Moses had no stomach for going through all that again. So, Moses, as the great leader he was, kept his little band out of the way (for forty years). But that really doesn't concern us here. Our focus is on the first twenty-five plus verses of Exodus, which we now have well in hand. To cope with the demands of the exercise, we will revert to the ancient technique of the Talmud (I think) of stating the text then adding descriptive notes to explain the whole thing, and let he/she who is without sin, cast the first stone.

---

7 Jean-Pierre Isbouts, *The Biblical World: An Illustrated Bible* (Toronto: National Geographic Society, 2007).

CHAPTER 2: GENESIS AND GEOLOGY 101

GENESIS IS CALLED THE first book of Moses, perhaps having something to do with the foregoing biased bit of narrative, but the following is an exceptionally realistic account, if one can get beyond the repetitive language of the biblical version and the geologic interpretation of time. Perhaps a handy way of bridging the gap is to incorporate my dear mother's perspective of the old line, which I think comes from the not so old, Anglican hymn "a thousand ages in thy sight are like an evening gone."

The first most remarkable congruence of the two sources is the biblical six days of creation and the six geological eras. (Don't quibble; the first era is not on the chart because there were no life forms).

Day 1: This is the time before we actually begin the geological calendar. So this "first time" includes the condensation of the nebula, the cooling of the primal earth, the condensation of the atmosphere, and formation of land and sea. Somewhere up to 10 billion years ago.

Day 2: The Archan—1,300 million years duration. There were probably some algae and bacteria in the oceans—at least in the latter part.

Day 3: The Proterozoic Era—1,930 million years duration. Some soft-bodied organisms and tube worms, again only in the oceans.

Day 4: The Palaeozoic Era—325 million years long. An explosion of life forms in the first period, the Cambrian, and then shellfish, coral, and fish in the ocean and coal beds formed on land.

Day 5: The Mesozoic Era—178.6 million years in duration. Land animals, reptiles, and dinosaurs.

Day 6: The Cennozoic Era: 66.4 million years long. Birds, mammals, and seed-bearing plants appeared.

The boundaries of these time units might be judged as arbitrary. There is not an exact fit between the biblical and scientific versions, but considering they are separated by thousands, even millions of years, there is an amazing congruence, if one can permit a little juggling of the order of the biblical presentation. There have been a number of attempts to do this, so I'm not claiming any originality, nor that all authors agree on exactly every point. I'm only saying that a very reasonable correlation can be achieved with a minimum of massaging. Perhaps the most important concept to get one's brain around is the six periods, whether one considers them to be days in the ordinary sense of the word or geological periods. The time before the sun ignited constitutes most of the first "day" in geological/astronomical terms, which most people, except for the real diehards, will concede must have been a very long time. From there, the geological concept of day is quite flexible and seems to relate more to what was happening on the planet, while the biblical version appears to stick to the earth's twenty-four-hour rotation, but does it really? We modern sophisticates have to bear in mind whom this was written for. First, of all, it wasn't written; it was handed down through the oral keepers of the tribal history, who made whatever modifications they deemed necessary. Secondly, the origins of much of it were probably from outside the tribe, from an entirely different culture. The biblical descriptions do not run very far afield of the geological, and the concept "day" appears to be more of a metaphor than any chronological time period. Who would have understood geological eras five thousand to seven thousand years ago? I don't quite understand them now. We have to bear in mind that those kinds of numbers didn't even exist in the human ken yet. The Arabic decimal system of numeration was millennia in the future. So my conclusion is that the biblical account is simply a superbly crafted metaphor for the then audience. Now, let's try to make sense of the metaphor.

The technique I will use is to quote the biblical version then comment on how it might be interpreted, so that it fits into the generally accepted geologic time scale. For those who wish to adhere to Bishop Usher's six-thousand-year time scale, so be it, except that they will have to drop the idea of the flood, because it had to have happened shortly after the glaciers melted some twelve thousand years ago. And we can definitely date that.

The First Book of Moses: Genesis (King James Version)

Bible	Geology 101
1. The History of Creation: In the beginning, God created the heavens and the earth.	The local galaxy and the thousands of other galaxies beyond were created after the big bang. One must include here the rather obvious afterthought from verse 16: "He made the stars also." This idea of bits and pieces out of order will continue to be a central idea in this interpretation and was explained through a bit of conjuring with respect to how this disorder may have actually come about.
2. The earth was without form, and void; and darkness was on the face of the deep. And the Spirit of God was hovering over the face of the waters.	"Without form" refers to the concept of the earth (et al.) being in the form of a "nebulae"—which is a cloud of dust and gas. Of course it was dark, because the sun had not yet ignited. Now put on your imaginative hat and hang on to it. We still don't know what gravity is, but here's as good a description as you are likely to encounter—"the Spirit of God" and it hovered over the face of the waters. Hovering is about as good a layman's description of the way gravity acts as would be likely anywhere and "the waters" is not a bad early metaphor for "particulate matter," i.e., minerals, compounds, and elements in the form of small particles. In other words—"gravity" (the Spirit of God) holds the universe together. Barring a better explanation, I can accept that.

3. Then God said: "Let there be light"; and there was light. 4. And God saw the light; that it was good; and God divided the light from the darkness. 5. God called the light Day, and the darkness He called Night. So the evening and the morning were the first day.	Well! You didn't expect to see the equations for nuclear fusion to be published for a gang of desert nomads now, did you? (The Iranians are still not allowed to have them.) But of course the sun eventually reached a critical mass and ignited the hydrogen to helium fusion process, and there was light—big time. It was still only the first day, remember (5,000–10,000 million years ago). The sun ignited before we could really detect much happening earth side, except to project that earth was probably there as a mass of rocky stuff.
6. Then God said: "Let there be a firmament in the midst of the waters, and let it divide the waters from the waters." 7. Thus God made the firmament, and divided the waters, which were under the firmament from the waters which were above the firmament; and it was so. 8. And God called the firmament Heaven. So the evening and the morning were the second day.	The problem here is one of semantics; firmament to us later-day types means something more solid than is implied here. But that was obviously not the meaning in this instance. One should probably interpret "the waters" as particulate matter (small particles of water, minerals, gases whatever) and firmament as a reference to the condensation of these particles. Though this had probably been going on for some time, it is presented to us here in a single lump. One probably shouldn't get their knickers in a knot over the wording. It seems as though the author is more or less talking about the atmosphere and the stratosphere or space, although some would like to include the oceans, which would probably be okay, because the dividing line given here appears to be the top of the clouds. This is only day 2, and we are just into the Achaean era, maybe.

9. Then God said: "Let the waters under the heavens be gathered together into one place, and let the dry land appear, and it was so. 10. And God called the dry land Earth, and gathering together of waters He called Seas. And God saw that it was good.	It is generally assumed that as the earth cooled down, the volatiles in the atmosphere, mostly water, were able to condense and fill the ocean basins. Of course, once there was water on the surface, erosion of the portions that weren't submerged provided the sediment from which the continents were built. Unfortunately, continental drift has been responsible for swallowing up that original continental stuff, so that nowhere is the original crust of the earth in evidence. The "dry land" of the biblical reference has long since been recycled. That does not mean that there is anything wrong with this biblical reference, but certainly we are now into the Achaean Era. And no, this was not Pangaea, though it probably was a super continent of which there may have been a number throughout geologic time. Enter the Egyptian army. "Run, run for your life, don't worry about those clay tablets. Save yourself." The Hebrews disappear into the reeds and the Egyptians get stuck in mud. Back we go the next day to pick up the scattered tablets, and we didn't get them in exactly the correct order. Verses 11, 12, and 13 belong in the future, and numbers 14 through 18 belong back with verses 3, 4, and 5. These five verses (14–18) are only a recap, so let's not get too upset with the order.

11. Then God said, "Let the earth bring forth grass, and herb that yields seed, and the fruit tree that yields fruit according to its kind, whose seed is in itself, on the earth"; and it was so. 12. And the earth brought forth grass, the herb that yields seed according to its kind, and the tree that yields fruit, whose seed is in itself according to its kind, and God saw that it was good. 13. So the evening and the morning were the third day.	Here is where we need the grass to feed, the cattle somewhere in the Cenozoic Era (day 6). Grass is actually a pretty modern item, pegged at 26 million years ago, and of course we had to have grass before we could have cattle. But it is a very notable juncture, just as the good book suggests. The evolution of seed-bearing plants was a major evolutionary breakthrough, as suggested. It is just out of order here.
14. Then God said, "Let there be lights in the firmament of the heavens to divide the day from the night; and let them be for signs and seasons, and for days and years; 15. And let them be for lights in the firmament of the heavens to give light on the earth," and it was so.	Verse 14 is very interesting, however, because we dwellers of the more northern latitudes have no difficulty knowing what season it is: frost, snow, leaves falling, etc. But closer to the equator this is not so; one month is pretty much like the next, until suddenly the rains come and you should have had your crops planted! So, we have a reference here to the need for astronomy to tell us when to plant, etc. (remember the Mayan astronomer/priests?)

16. Then God made two great lights; the greater light to rule the day, and the lesser light to rule the night. He made the stars also. 17. God set them in the firmament of the heavens to give light on the earth, 18. and to rule over the day and over the night, and to divide the light from the darkness. And God saw that it was good. 19. So the evening and the morning were the fourth day.	In Verse 16, I previously mentioned the line at the end as an afterthought. I guess that because we are talking about lights in the heavens, we should probably mention the stars. But it does look suspiciously as if that is the origin of this little addition. It seems simply appended because we are talking about lights in the heavens. We haven't mentioned the stars before, so we had better say something about them. It now seems like it is probably a later addition to fix up a perceived omission (the editor probably didn't get paid).
20. Then God said: "Let the waters abound with an abundance of living creatures, and let birds fly above the earth across the face of the firmament of the heavens. 21. So God created great sea creatures and every living thing that moves, with which the waters abounded, according to their kind, and every winged bird according to its kind. And God saw that it was good. 22. And God blessed them, saying, "Be fruitful and multiply and fill the waters in the seas, and let birds multiply on the earth 23. So the evening and the morning were the fifth day.	Verses 20 and 21 are getting a little carried away. Yes, the waters of the Paleozoic do "abound with an abundance of living creatures," but the birds aren't due for probably 250 million years yet. Besides, we're getting ahead of ourselves; we're still in day 4. Lots of fish but no birds. We must wait for day 6 for them. So from verse 20 to 25, some surgery will be required to sort out that which belongs to day 5 (the Mesozoic) and day 6 (the Cenozoic).

24. Then God said, "Let the earth bring forth the living creature according to its kind: cattle and creeping thing and beast of the earth, each according to its kind": and it was so. 25. And God made the beast of the earth according to its kind, cattle according to its kind, and everything that creeps on the earth according to its kind. And God saw that it was good.	Verses 24 and 25 belong in day 6 and do make oblique reference to creepy crawlies, i.e., lizards, reptiles, et al. There is no sense in mentioning dinosaurs, because no one would know what they were, and of course, birds were dinosaurs anyway. The problem appears to centre around day 6 being sort of reserved for the creation of man and his needs being met. This is okay, but this is where the birds belong too.
26. Then God said, "Let us make man in Our image, according to Our likeness; let them have dominion over the fish of the sea, over the birds of the air, and over the cattle, over all the earth and over every creeping thing that creeps on the earth.	Why are *we* making man in *our* image? Why the plural? But it could be satisfied if the plural were just the idea of the weak force and the strong force (that's where the movies got the idea), and just perhaps it is actually looking forward to this era when we might understand that "God" could be the force (gravitation?) that underpins everything. At least, probably not the medieval grandfather image, but more likely it is something in the scribes understanding like multiple gods.
27. So God created man in His own image; in the image of God He created him; male and female He created them.	In Verse 27 "He created him, male and female." Adam's rib is not mentioned here, so presumably this was added at a later time by a somewhat more chauvinistic author, whose mommy and daddy had never sat him down and talked about the birds and the bees.

28. Then God blessed them, and God said to them: "Be fruitful and multiply; fill the earth and subdue it; have dominion over the fish of the sea, over the birds of the air, and over every living thing that moves on the earth.	The admonition to fill the earth, subdue it, and have dominion over everything could certainly be construed as developing the big brain, which would make all of that possible, a sort of "stand and deliver" stance once the higher level of intelligence had been imbued through the mechanism of glaciation. This sort of left out the poor old Neanderthals, though. I guess they were on the wrong side of the intellectual divide.
29. And God said, "See, I have given you every herb that yields seed which is on the face of all the earth, and every tree whose fruit yields seed; to you it shall be for food. 30. Also, to every beast of the earth, to every bird of the air, and to everything that creeps on the earth, in which there is life, I have given every green herb for food"; and it was so. 31. Then God saw everything that He had made, and indeed it was very good. So the evening and the morning were the sixth day.	Interesting that there is even a reference to the evolution of flowering and seed bearing plants in the Cenozoic (day 6).

1. Thus the heavens and the earth, and all that host of them, were finished. 2. And on the seventh day God ended His work which He had done, and He rested on the seventh day from all His work which He had done. 3. Then God blessed the seventh day and sanctified it, because in it He rested from all His work which God had created and made. 4. This is the history of the heavens and the earth when they were created, in the day that the Lord God made the earth and the heavens; 5. before any plant of the field was in the earth and before any herb of the field had grown. For the Lord God had not caused it to rain on the earth, and there was no man to till the ground; 6. but a mist went up from the earth and watered the whole face of the ground.	Chapter 2, day 7, "the day of rest," seems also to have been a day of reflection, as we are transported back to verse 27 of the previous chapter to put a little "flesh on the bones" with verses 2 to 5 here, the advent of weather somewhere back before or at the beginning of the Archean, when the earth was cool enough for the water cycle to establish.

7. And the Lord God formed man of the dust of the ground, and breathed into his nostrils the breath of life; and man became a living being.[1]	Then of course, the familiar "from dust to dust," with which few will argue. And, can you find fault with this little diatribe? Of course you can, but that is not really the point. Where on earth (or heaven) did anyone ever come up with all of this stuff thousands of years ago? What is the significance of such a lengthy comparison? One can look at it from a number of different vantage points or points of view: (a) Were all geologists simply brought up in the grand tradition of the Anglican faith?—Probably not; but it would prove a simple solution, or (b) did God simply set some Egyptian scribes down and dictate a list of historic evolution to them?—it is certainly an intriguing idea! Or, (c) did some little blue men out in the Sahara actually figure it all out and their multiple musings somehow get collected in the world's first centre of learning in the Nile delta (my personal choice). Or, (d) It's all a bunch of hogwash and the author should be referred to a competent psychologist!

So, where does all of this leave us? Well, it kind of depends on your own orientation. Personally, I was brought up in the Anglican persuasion and the old prelate, Mr. Saunders, might be proud of giving the Good Book good, solid scientific support. But I'm going with the little blue men out in the desert (like, what did "I" give you that big brain for, if it wasn't to figure things out?) See "Glaciation" below for the little blue men saga.

Personally, I am comfortable with a deity who looks out for me (provided that I behave), but I'm not allowed to "cop out" and take the easy exit by putting all the responsibility onto "Him." Maybe he kick-started the whole thing, but I'm left in charge to husband the earth and the vicissitudes of its denizens so that they don't set fire to the whole structure. To that end, I've been allocated this big brain in order to figure it all out. How am a doing? Well, so far, not too well! That's why the book I wrote provides more background to attempt to use modern geology to search out some of the scientific background for our persistent legends and scriptures. However, before embarking on that quest, we did promise the Geology 101 students a more cogent, rational, and ordinal view of these first twenty-six verses of the Good Book, if only to reassure ourselves that we might be truly up to the task of placing such a treasure above the dismissal it has so often been accorded. Perhaps the class might be sufficiently forgiving to permit the odd explanatory note when we do not truly know what we are talking about. In any case, beloved students, here is our best effort.

DAY 1: BIG BANG and Galaxies
GENESIS
1:1   In the beginning, God created the heavens and the earth.
1:2   The earth was without form, and void; and darkness was on the face of the deep. And the Spirit of God was hovering over the face of the waters.
1:6   Then God said, "Let there be a firmament in the midst of the waters, and let it divide the waters from the waters."
1:7   Thus God made the firmament, and divided the waters, which were under the firmament from the waters which were above the firmament; and it was so.
1:14   Then God said "Let there be lights in the firmament of the heavens to divide the day from the night; and let them be for signs and seasons, and for days and years;
1:5   God called the light Day, and the darkness He called Night. So the evening and the morning were the first day.

DAY 2: CREATION OF the Solar System

1:16   Then God made two great lights; the greater light to rule the day, and the lessser light to rule the night. He made the stars also.
1:3   Then God said: "Let there be light"; and there was light.

1:17   God set them in the firmament of the heavens to give light on the earth.

1:4   And God saw the light; that it was good; and God divided the light from the darkness.

1:15   And let them be for lights in the firmament of the heavens to give light on the earth, and it was so.

1:18   And to rule over the day and over the night, and to divide the light from the darkness. And God saw that it was good.

1:8   And God called the firmament Heaven. So the evening and the morning were the second day.

DAY 3: THE PRECAMBRIAN

1:9   Then God said: "Let the waters under the heavens be gathered together into one place, and let the dry land appear and it was so.

1:10   And God called the dry land Earth, and gathering together of waters He called Seas. And God saw it was good.

1:13   So the evening and the morning were the third day.

DAY 4: THE PALEOZOIC

1:20   Then God said: "Let the waters abound with an abundance of living creatures."

1:21   So God created great sea creatures and every living thing that moves, with which the waters abounded, according their kind,

1:19   So the evening and the morning were the fourth day

DAY 5: THE MESOZOIC

1:11   Then God said, "Let the earth bring forth grass, the herb that yields seed, and the fruit tree that yields fruit according to its kind, whose seed is in itself, on the earth"; and it was so.

1:12   And the earth brought forth grass, the herb that yields seed according to its kind, and the tree that yields fruit, whose seed is in itself according to its kind. And God saw that it was good

1:20   and let the birds fly above the earth across the face of the firmament of the heavens

1:21   and every winged bird according to it's kind, And God saw that it was good

1:22   and God blessed them, saying, "Be fruitful and multiply, fill the waters in the seas, and let birds multiply on the earth.

1:24   Then God said, "Let the earth bring forth the living creature according to its kind: cattle and creeping thing and beast of the earth, each according to its kind": and it was so.

1:25   And God made the beast of the earth according to its kind, cattle according to its kind, and everything that creeps on the earth according to its kind. And God saw that it was good.

1:23   So the evening and the morning were the fifth day.

DAY 6: THE CENOZOIC

1:26   Then God said, "Let Us make man in Our image, according to Our likeness; let them have dominion over the fish of the sea, over the birds of the air, and over the cattle, over all the earth and over every creeping thing that creeps on the earth

1:27   So God created man in His own image, in the image of God He created him; male and female He created them.

1:28   Then God blessed, them, and God said to them, "Be fruitful and multiply; fill the earth and subdue it; have dominion over the fish of the sea, over the birds of the air, and over every living thing that moves on the earth

1:29   And God said, "See, I have given you every herb that yields seed which is on the face of all the earth, and every tree whose fruit yields seed; to you it shall be for food

1:30   Also, to every beast of the earth, to every bird of the air, and to everything that creeps on the earth, in which there is life, I have given every green herb for food"; and it was so.

1:31   Then God saw everything that He had made, and indeed it was very good. So the evening and the morning were the sixth day.

One might be forgiven if they thought that they saw something different in these last six verses. The style is certainly different—even the wording seems significantly different—so one might suspect a different source. That would not be at all surprising, as the subject matter changes from geology/palaeontology to some very significant distant relatives of ours, namely Adam and Eve, although apparently in this version they were created equal with no recourse to ribcage magic.

Well, "God bless us everyone." What might the existence of this ancient geological knowledge have to do with anything? Well, first of all, we "moderns" should probably tuck in the frayed edges of our superiority complexes and admit that we are not the first down this road. That admission really does set the stage to sort of disrupt our narcissistic navel gazing and jerk the reality chain. If this kind of in-depth geo/astro understanding existed probably before the ice melted, then there must be a lot more of it around somewhere. The reader may remark on my snivelling plea for a submersible as the mere whining of a spoilt brat or the insidious underpinnings for another book (all of the above!). There is presently not enough information around to write that next book, so I must content myself with picking up a few loose terrestrial scraps in order to put a little flesh on the bones of the "above sea level" part of the yarn.

Thanks, Moses. Were it not for your prosaic commitment, we would not even have this toehold on which to speculate. So I'll see what I can do with the geology of the legends.

QUESTIONS

1. I suppose that Moses' parentage will always be a question, but was he educated in Alexandria or did Alexandria come to the Egyptian palace?
2. Who were the scribes who inscripted the twelve tablets? Certainly not Hebrew bond slaves.
3. Where on earth was the origin of those first twenty-five verses of Geneses? It is easy to believe that the information came from the libraries of Alexandria, but where did they get it?
4. Is there any other information, perhaps kicking around in other sacred texts, that might shed some light on the origin of the first twenty-five verses?

5. After forty years in the desert, where did this Hebrew tribe locate when they were suffered to return to the promised land—the West Bank? (Read Isbouts *Biblical World*)[8]

---

8 Jean-Pierre Isbouts, *The Biblical World: An Illustrated Bible* (Toronto: National Geographic Society, 2007).

CHAPTER 3:   GLACIATION
(THE HANDMAIDEN OF GOD)

LAUNCHING INTO THE SECONDARY topic of glaciation may seem a little strange to some. Geologists will immediately twig, "It's the melt-water, not the ice." They would be correct to a certain extent, but glaciation has so many subsidiary nuances that we must stop a bit along the way to consider the profound implications of that little quirk in the weather. The repercussions due to the retreat of the glaciers will be implicated in the Geology chapter as the primal mechanism for world flooding. The tales of catastrophy are so 'intimately' bound up with this world event that we should attempt to feel comfortable and accept what a meaningful mechanism such a global event as glaciation has been in our assention to world supremacy.

There are basically four items for consideration:

1. How it all came about (some history of the earth)
2. What impact it had on our distant ancestors (evolution)
3. How the "great melt" created persistent legends (anthropology and religion)
4. "It ain't over yet" (global warming and the flip of the conveyor)

The Pleistocene and subsequent glaciations have been going on for some 2.5 million years. Glaciation waxes and wanes, but it never goes away, and it spans the period of much of human evolution, from a funny looking little ape to the classy persona that we see today. The relationship seems to many to be something more than accidental, but perhaps it is not. In whatever the case, it was our evolved species that faced the cataclysm that gave rise to the flood stories. We will use modern geological insights to put flesh on the bones of what has often been dismissed as a myth. But the tale is real, and very much a part of our heritage, as are—at least portions of—the biblical take on the subject in the book of Genesis. From my perspective, we all need to understand a little bit more about glaciation and its profound implications in order to better appreciate what a colossal work we humans actually are and how we got to this point, let alone some of our missing artefacts. God probably didn't gesture hypnotically to create man; he probably used the materials available—in all probability it was a long-term project, not just an isolated incident.

It is somewhat difficult to talk to Canadians and northern Europeans about glaciation, because they live with the physical aftermath on a daily basis. They take a sort of "ho hum, but will it grow roses?" attitude. This is not so with many Americans and Mediterraneans, who tend to evince real interest. ("Really? You don't say! A mile thick—astounding!") So you can just imagine that when Louis Agassiz (a Swiss geologist) declared he saw many of the same structures on the plains of Europe that he saw in the Alps, it was not an easy sell. "This is just the way it is and always has been." But sell the concept he did, and for his trouble he had the great humungous glacial lake in Manitoba, Ontario, and North Dakota named after him (Lake Winnipeg, Lake Winnipegosis, and the flood plain of the Red River now occupy the site of this immense glacial melt water lake: Agassiz). But that is how it was. Everything was so huge that it staggers the imagination. I live right in the basin of Glacial Lake, Calgary, and just a couple of kilometres away from where the mountain glacier ran into the great continental glacier. Actually, it's a little more complicated than that, but I have never ceased being amazed at all the artefacts of these giant ice dozers.

Therefore, it is little wonder that people have difficulty projecting the climatic effects down onto the plains of Africa. But as Moslems are so fond of saying, "God is Great." It is just that our puny little minds—with nothing to compare it to—have not caught up with the scale of the thing. So it is with a bit of hesitation and trepidation that I presume to plough ahead with the tale as I see it. Certainly I am no expert, but glacial geologists are hard to come by, so you will have to put up with my feeble efforts until perhaps one of those smart guys feel moved to fill in the detail and set the record straight. You are not required to agree with anything, but do formulate questions as to how all of this relates to anything.

Most readers of this tome will have heard of continental drift, but few perhaps, know what it is, much less have connected it with other freaky stuff like glaciation. Most people know that the two exist, but other than the global warming scare, have little interest. The purpose of all the speculation in this tract is to interest laypersons in speculation with regards to what happened to the earth and us in the past few million years, in order to pose astute questions to all of those smart guys who are supposed to know these things.

The story is indeed intriguing and following up on the impact on "us" of such far-out geological folderol can be seen as very impressive. But as one wag put it, "You mean that continental drift has anything to do with our tenure here on the planet?"

The continents kind of "float" on a semi-liquid called magma in that portion of the earth under its solid outer shell or crust, called the mantle. Magma is like very hot porridge with partially formed crystals floating around in some as yet uncrystalized stuff. The continents are movable by convection currents within the earth that help to keep its internal heat distributed, so that when the hot semi-molten stuff moves under the continents, it moves the continents too.

North and South America are slowly drifting west at about the same rate as your fingernails grow, so we don't normally notice it on a daily basis and are inclined to ignore it. But if you live in Vancouver, British Columbia, Canada, it gets a bit more critical, because it causes earthquakes—really big ones similar to those in Haiti, Chile, Turkey, or Indonesia. Again, it was not until the international geophysical year produced the intricate evidence that we understood what was happening under our feet.

For considerable time, though, it had been noticed on maps of the world that North and South America seemed to fit neatly into Africa and Europe like pieces of a jigsaw puzzle, with Central America being the laggard piece. One can see on the map that the Central American piece of the puzzle has a comma and reverse comma shape indicative of "dragging its feet" between North and South America. As the Atlantic Ocean opened wider and wider, over some 200 million years, entirely new ocean currents had to develop in order to distribute the heat in the ocean (standard convection currents of Physics 101).

Warm water from the tropics moved north forming the Gulf Stream, keeping Europe much warmer than it might otherwise have been. The cold, salty, dense Arctic water sinks to the ocean floor and moves south down the east coast of North America and east of the mid-Atlantic ridge. Those warm and cold currents are usually referred to as the Atlantic Conveyor by climatologists. The Gulf Stream is pretty evident on the surface, but the return leg traveling south at depths is little noticed. Again it is a classic convection cell.

The Atlantic conveyor is what keeps the climate stable on both sides of the Atlantic; disrupt that by dumping in an excess of low-gravity fresh meltwater into the northern reaches of the Atlantic, and you will do a number on the climate (see "The Little Ice Age").

It may have been marginally more complex that that 3 to 4 million years ago, because the Isthmus of Panama had not yet emerged (remember the laggard Central American block), and there was still an exchange of water between the Atlantic and Pacific through the Panama gap. All of that ended when the Isthmus of Panama emerged. It probably wrecked havoc on El Nino and La Nina, or just the opposite: it could have created these climatic effects. In all probability, though, through all of that interrelated climatic stuff, "the gap" figured largely in keeping the earth's climate in some sort of tenuous balance. When the Isthmus emerged and shut off the circulation, all hell broke loose. It may have taken hundreds of thousands of years to sort itself out. Evaporative cooling of the warm Gulf Stream added a lot of moisture to the northern hemisphere and the intensification of the Gulf Stream will have postponed the onset of the ice age for a while (see page 250 of *A Brain for All Seasons,* by W. H. Calvin).[9] The detail has still to be worked out, but gradually the north became moister and colder and the southern latitudes hotter and drier. Gradually more precipitation in the form of snow fell over the northern latitudes in the winter than could melt during the summers, and it began to compress into ice. At its maximum, the ice over Canada, Europe, and Russia was over a mile thick, and it moved downhill.

I shan't get into calculating the Coriolis force of the rotating earth, which was instrumental in moving the colossal mass of matter (i.e., ice) in somewhat the same fashion as it does masses of cold arctic air out of the north to form the cold fronts that we call "outbreaks of Arctic air." Well, just imagine if it was ice! If you wish to see how the Coriolis force works, smear some sticky liquid around the north pole of a ball and rotate the ball (just don't do it in the front room). I don't suspect that I have to explain what happened to the ice. It moved south, grinding up everything in its path.

Over the several millions of years of the Pleistocene and Pliocene glaciations, there have been at least four major global warming periods. In addition, ice core samples from the Arctic, along with sea bed core samples taken off the East and West Coasts, suggest that there may have been sixteen or more minor global warming periods. Each succeeding glacial maxima erased most of the evidence for the previous one, so you really have to know what you are doing to track these things. The flooding that occurred when the ice melted was prodigious, washing away most of the evidence that might have survived the bulldozing action of the ice (see *Glacial Lake Missoula and Its Humongous Floods,* by David Alt).[10]

But don't confuse this terrestrial flooding with Noah's cataclysmic experience. That was an entirely different scenario, though marginally related.

One of the more dynamic features of all the climactic change of the glacial period was the wind. Granted, the normal weather patterns would have been severely disrupted and when the big thaws happened the weather probably didn't know what hit it. But why the

9 William H. Calvin, *A Brain for all Seasons: Human Evolution and Abrupt Climate Change* (Chicago: University of Chicago Press, 2002), 250.
10 David Alt, *Glacial Lake Missoula and Its Humongous Floods* (Missoula: Mountain Press Publishing, 2001).

big winds? How do we know these winds occurred? Winds blow from high pressure (cold) to low pressure (hot) and the differentials must have been immense and every changing as the ice ebbed and flowed. In northeastern Saskatchewan, one can walk all day along a single sand dune. It's not quite that dramatic in Eastern Europe, but there is considerable evidence of extremely high winds over a long period.

The ebbing and flowing of glacial pulses appear to be related to what the earth is doing in its orbit around the sun. Because global warming is such a hot topic just now, we probably should mention the Milankovich cycles. Although they are not responsible for glaciations, they are to blame for the waxing and waning cycles that modify the effects of glaciations every 22,000, 41,000, and 100,000 years. The 100,000-year period results from the gravity of the other planets (when in alignment) pulling the earth's orbit out of its normally (almost) circular configuration into an ellipse. This brings the earth closer to the sun on the flat side of the ellipse. The 22,000-year pulse occurs because the angle of inclination of the earth's axis toward the sun changes over time. The more it tilts toward the sun, the more the sun warms the northern latitudes. The 41,000-year figure is due to the fact that the earth does not rotate evenly around its own axis; it wobbles, thus creating greater inclination toward the sun at sometimes than at other times. We call the average tilt the angle of inclination, which we have already indicated, is itself variable. In addition, the sun itself has a fifteen-hundred-year-cycle of waxing and waning energy output, appropriately called the fifteen-hundred-year cycle. The eleven-year sunspot cycle, which most people know about, doesn't do much in the way of temperature change; it just blasts our poor ol' benighted planet with high energy charged particles which we call the solar wind, which can play havoc with the power grids but give us gorgeous northern lights. Then, of course, we add to the whole mess by spewing greenhouse gases into the atmosphere, which probably helps to speed up the whole warming process, and once the whole warming thing gets going, it feeds on itself, until finally it will probably disrupt the Atlantic conveyor and we get plunged back into a "little ice age." C'est la vie. I won't be around for that one! The most recent of these latter cycles probably started prior to 800 AD, followed by what is commonly known as the Little

Ice Age. This leads us to assume that the next one is probably not due for at least 200 more years. (I am certain a degree in physics and astronomy would be helpful in predicting the next occurrence, so I won't attempt to display any insight at this time, with the exception of noting that we don't have a very good reading on the margin of error + or – in that 1,500-year figure.)

I don't know to which orbital or solar event the astronomers might assign the most recent four-hundred-year warming period (800–1221 AD), but it was an eventful time on the planet. In Europe, it was warm and the earth shed its bounty on its inhabitants. Crops were full, people prospered, and the feudal Middle Ages with the lords and serfs became a time of architectural glory. Many beautiful cathedrals were built to prove or celebrate their gratitude to the Almighty. Optimism was so high that the Danes even established an agricultural colony on the west coast of Greenland—which lasted over four hundred years. Compare that with the young life of the settlement of the North American continent of five hundred years!

History has that damnable habit of repeating itself. (Read Jared Diamond's *Collapse*.)[11] As previously mentioned, we should not have been due for another "sun pulse" warming for two hundred years—unless, of course, some unforeseen event occurred to help speed up the whole process. At the same time that Europe was enjoying its prosperous time, elsewhere on the planet times were not so great. It was certainly warm! The high priests of the Mayan culture had maintained their exalted positions because they had an "in" with the gods and could predict exactly when the rains would come, and so they dictated the planting of the crops. The plebes, in awe of such extraterrestrial connections, were beholden to the priestly class. However, the priests were astronomers and their other worldly connections amounted to perhaps nothing more than keeping an accurate calendar, taking note of the seasonal rains and so forth. Eventually, when the rains didn't come, they lost their prestige, and Mayan society came apart. It was inevitable though, as the success of the Mayan society was so great that the number of citizens soon began to exceed the ability of the land to sustain so

---

11 Jared Diamond, *Collapse: How Societies Choose to Fail or Succeed* (Toronto: Viking, 2005).

many—a fine example of the Malthusian cycle (good times promote increased population which eventually outstrips the ability of the land to support it). The drought provided a tipping point for the demise of the Mayan culture. There is, however, a very interesting modern sequel to the Mayan disaster that reaches into the present day. Certain doomsday prophets have used the end of the Mayan calendar to predict the end of days based on nothing more than that the Mayan priests couldn't go on printing out their calendar forever, so stopped at quitting time in the month of squirting Quinine in the year of the Rabbit, which just happens to translate to 2012. But there is a buck to be made here. We can rent space in old missile silos and under various rocks for the true believers to weather the apocalypse. Personally, I think that that is being pretty presumptive, because if God wanted to end the whole experiment, He would not resort to half measures (remember that He did it once before). And bear in mind that those Mayan priests were incapable of predicting their own demise. So no, the end is not nigh, at least not for that reason.

Further to the east, in Asia, the Steppes of Mongolia were drying out, and Genghis Khan successfully invaded China (1213–1215 AD) and eventually invaded and took over parts of Europe. In 1221 or thereabouts, the rains came to Europe, and it rained for six years. Was this the Atlantic conveyor doing its celebrated and expected flip? It is hard to say, as oceanographic monitoring stations were nonexistent. Europe however was devastated. There were virtually no crops, and the population was starving. Malnutrition made the citizens easy targets for disease such as the bubonic plague and various other plague bearing bacteria. Just to add insult to injury, the Little Ice Age descended on Europe. Is this then, actual proof of the flip of the Atlantic Conveyor, wherein the Gulf Stream no longer bathed Europe in its warm embrace? Although we have no direct evidence, the mechanics do seem obvious. It had happened once before, in fairly recent geologic history. That period is called the Younger Dryas (after a relative to the rose that is adapted to grow in sub arctic conditions). For this period, we have a little more direct empirical evidence. It happened some 10,500 years ago and is believed to have been the result of the breaking up of the ice dam that held the fresh water in Lake Aggasiz that immense melt water lake on the eastern prairies. A flood of cold, fresh water surged across the Great Lakes, down the St. Lawrence River, out across the Gulf of St. Lawrence, and mixed with the warm waters of the Gulf Stream, disrupting it and knocking the Atlantic Conveyor for a loop. The Conveyor didn't recover for centuries, and neither did the weather.

Actually, the younger Dryas occurred just when hunter-gatherers were experimenting with settling down in proto-agricultural communities in the Middle East. Ian Morris (*Why the West Rules – For Now*, p. 101–107)[12] draws attention to settlements east of the Jordan River in what he calls the Hilly Flanks, which were probably or partially abandoned in the cold dry snap of the Younger Dryas 10,500–9,500 years ago. They reappeared when the climate returned to normal. Somewhat the same thing may have happened on the north-western shelf of the Black Sea, only the subsequent flooding puts all of the evidence under water. Oooops! We are getting ahead of our own story. Sorry about that!

Something about this sounds vaguely familiar. You don't suppose that Al Gore is some sort of prophet? What would prophets have sounded like to an unaware public? Perhaps just the opposite, if he might be seen as obstructing God's plan for our next big mutation. Fast forward to the item on domestication speeding up adaption. What bigger occasion of bringing us to heel than jerking the climate chain, as we get swelled heads over all of this e-space thing. Looks pretty suspicious to me!

Some very devout people of a scientific persuasion maintain that glaciation is very simply God's chosen instrument for how *He* wishes to see *His* chosen handiwork to eventually turn out—a work in progress, so to speak. Personally, I don't see much wrong with that model if one can only refrain from telling the deity what He will and will not be permitted to do and with what tools. One can't help but reflect, on this point for the great intellectual battle of the nineteenth century. Einstein, generally accused of determinism, said, "God doesn't play dice," which was a snide reference to the scientific

---

12 Morris, *Why the West Rules - For Now:* (McClelland & Steward, 2011), 101–107.

opposition of *Quantum Mechanics* led by Neils Bohr, who countered with the concept of probability and retorted to the Master, "Stop telling God what he can and cannot do—He's God!"

Perhaps all this conjecturing is just narrative fallacy (see the *Black Swan* by Nassim Talib).[13] I think that a little humility is in order to enjoy the sense of wonder at this fascinating and fantastic tale. But we humans aren't very good at being humble. Enough conjecture, back to the main story.

Some four to seven million years ago, *Australopithecus* split off from our chimpanzee forbearer lineage to become a separate species. This new little guy on the block was rather strange looking, standing upright, and perhaps only four feet tall—a half-man/half-ape who was able to run upright and forage effectively on the veldt but also able to scamper up the nearest tree whenever a predator approached. The birthday of the new species is somewhat clouded by time, but glaciation did not play a role in the species survival at this point. However, 1.5–2 million years ago, a more robust upright descendant appeared on the African savannas, and we call him *Homo habalis*. Glaciation most certainly played an important role in the creation and disappearance of this species. This is where the pace quickens, and this is well within the onset of glaciation farther north and the intense drying out of the African plains, because the glaciers had much of the water trapped in ice up north. Lightning strikes ignited numerous prairie fires on the drought-ridden savannas, and *habalis* took advantage of the roasted carcasses left behind by the grass fires. He eventually figured out a way to light his own fires (sticks or flints?) and thereby helped to secure his existence on earth. Protein feeds the brain, and *habalis's* cerebellum kept growing, because one absorbs more protein from cooked food. He began to play around with different shaped rocks and invented simple tools such as the hand axe and hide scraper. The hand axe was good for cracking bones and getting at the marrow—a concentrated source of brain-building protein. The *habalis* forehead began to evolve with all of that good protein, and soon *Homo erectus* appeared. Since the females preferred the high foreheads, with which to be seen at the opera, the bigger brained guys got preferred treatment,

---

13 Nassim Talib, *The Black Swan* (Mississauga: Random House, 2010)

and low foreheads fell out of fashion. Unfortunately, the good that the drought brought *erectus* was soon surpassed by the evil it also brought. Game became scarce, and erectus followed what little game there was to greener pastures. Some groups chose to stay put rather than follow the herds; however, the bulk of the population was on the move—following the migrating animals to pastures unknown. They didn't stop their move until they reached China and Indonesia. Voila, the appearance of Peking and Java man far away from Africa.

Most (many?) people today accept the thesis that man originated in Africa, but perhaps on little definitive evidence other than that is where the great apes are: a sort of tacit acceptance of relationship. We perhaps neglect to remember that the old man of the jungle, the orangutan, resides in Indonesia. So how did "he" get there? Well, perhaps Java man brought him along as a pet. But all silliness aside, why do we say that man originated in Africa? There used to be a theory that sort of played around with the idea of multiple origins, but no more. Why? Well, for the same reason as that we humans have a much smaller gene pool than the great apes—we almost "had the biscuit." We were mostly exterminated by climate change. Not so the apes who were lounging around in the jungle in their hammocks gorging on bananas and all sorts of other jungle delicacies whilst we were grubbing for roots, insects, and fresh water clams just to stay alive over on the savannas, and most of us didn't—stay alive, that is. That little setback reduced our gene pool significantly. It was as if the fittest survived and they were all relatives of big Moe. Now add to that the tiny little groups who came to the conclusion that they were mad as hell and not going to take it anymore, so took off toward the rising sun. Well, just as today, it would be very small groups who were of the same political persuasion, so when they packed up to leave the old homeland for greener pastures, they were too few to take a whole spectrum of genes with them, so they left all of that diversity behind. They only had a small packet of genes because each of these migrant groups was so small. Perhaps that's why we're all such a bunch of twits.

Apparently, the same thing applies to language. According to Dr. Quentin Atkinson of the University of Auckland in New Zealand (as reported in Science and Technology *The Economist* April 16, 2011), *"one of the lines of evidence which show humanities' African origins is that the farther you get from that continent, the less diverse, genetically speaking, people are".* They are descended from small groups of relatively recent migrants and are more inbred than their African forbearers because of their willingness to move. We'll call them Homo Adventurers.

For those who stayed behind, times got really tough. Two hundred thousand years ago the population dropped to perhaps ten thousand souls located somewhere around the coast of Tanzania, Kenya, or Somalia, or conceivably in the Rift Valley, or recently discovered on the south coast of Africa. The results for the existing species of man who remained in Africa varied. The loss of body hair helped the species cope with the intense heat, as they were probably situated very near the equator at the time, but man narrowly avoided extinction altogether. Our survival may have been the result of aforementioned abundant aquatic food from the Rift Lakes or the seashore. Again, so much good protein in such food could have been responsible for man's survival and helped to deflect our imminent extinction. The result of such high protein foods is to be found in the evolution of brain cells. The genetic change was astronomical. What is oft referred to as Mitochondrial Eve was invented (or cleverly crafted) and living in Somalia some two hundred thousand years ago—long before the Garden of Eden in Eastern Turkey. The eastern branch of man over in China and Java seems to have disappeared at this time. There is some evidence to show that they may have persisted as *Homo erectus* in Outer Mongolia up to fifty thousand years ago. The forbearers of Somalia/Kenya/Tanzania were more prominent in the evolutionary struggle.

The concept of Mitochondrial Eve needs some explanation, and I will attempt it as best I can.

The mitochondria are an internal portion of the cell DNA that supplies the cell with energy. Roughly one quarter of the energy that we humans use to run ourselves is required to run our big brains. The reasoning goes that when we underwent that monumental change from small-brained *Homo erectus* to large-brained *Homo sapiens*, something had to happen to the mitochondria to increase the energy output. These new, high-powered mitochondria were passed on only through the female gene—thereby giving us Mitochondrial Eve—the progenitor of modern man. The ancients seemed to have known and revered the importance of the female gender. That is hardly surprising, as the female of any species produce the subsequent generations. If you look at the gender of the ancient gods, it reflected the reality happening on earth. Perhaps that is why modern "man" seems to be in so much trouble—we have stopped listening to our right-brained goddesses—the women. Did the Bible perhaps get it backward as a result of the male-dominated society? Rather than Eve being created out of Adam's rib, was Adam created out of Eve's mitochondria?

There is a titillating little overtone here: despite our overriding male bravado, we have always known that women held the key. We shall return to this theme later when we consider the Hebrew version of Eve. Perhaps we revert to allegory when unsure of our sources or position. Scientific types could see the requirement for a change in the mitochondria, so they patched together the idea of Mitochondrial Eve as a proposition, not a proof, and many in the scientific community do not agree with it. For those with an urge to further their knowledge on this critical time in human history, I recommend W. H. Calvins's book *A Brain for All Seasons*.[14]

Success often seems to breed failure at another level, and so, for whatever reason, *Homo sapiens* also began to roam the land. However it was not until the years between 100,000–60,000 BC that there is proof of *Homo sapiens* wandering. This species of man roamed as far away as Australia, crossing a strait of water that is now 60 miles wide. How did they know that they weren't sailing off the edge of the world? There seems to have been an innate sense of astronomical knowledge. Author Jared Diamond in his book *Collapse*[15] goes on to explain how the Polynesians settled the Pacific Islands much later via astronomical knowledge of the stars, traveling in vessels possibly made of bamboo or balsa. The previous African exodus was completed during the time of the coming of

14 William H. Calvin, *A Brain for all Seasons: Human Evolution and Abrupt Climate Change:* (Chicago: University of Chicago Press, 2002).
15 Diamond, Jared, C*ollapse: How Societies Choose to Fail or Succeed* (Toronto: Viking, 2005).

consciousness, so perhaps "abject fear" had not yet been encoded. Compared to these mystic travelers, the Garden of Eden is a pretty bland story. Although to have the ancient oral traditionalists record the actual coming of consciousness in the Garden of Eden story is nothing short of amazing.

It is true, I think, that no one has actually proposed a definitive solution to the vexing question: How did *Homo sapiens* gain consciousness? Yes, I know: syntax. But then how and why syntax? No one has attempted to supply some upgraded version of "The Tree of Knowledge" in the Garden of Eden story. We don't seem to have a clue about what happened or why. Somehow there was an improved inter-cranial connection. But, how, why, and worldwide remains a question. *Homo sapiens* had possibly reached Australia by this time, or at least were on their way or perhaps the event, whatever it was, scattered them, like chaff before the wind. Well, the thesis of this chapter is that glaciation was the Handmaiden of God, but so far we've just sort of referred to the Big Ice as if it were the 800-pound gorilla in the room; we have not looked very carefully at some of its more obscure nuances nor other stuff that might have been going on to add to the scenario. So perhaps one should look to one's own thesis for answers or at least on the cutting room floor.

Now this is going to take, if not a suspension of belief, then at least a considerable stretch. So I'm only asking for consideration of a *way-out* hypothesis. Just remember the statement in defence of quantum mechanics: "Don't be telling God what he can or can't do". We've accepted the thesis that God may have used glaciation up north to cause drought down south, to expand man's cerebral capacity, producing *Homo sapiens* after millennia of sticking it to our ancestors with no insignificant loss of life, in order to refine this handiwork. Truly a jealous God, if you will, but certainly a determined one. Now we have this semi-intelligent ape out on the savannas of Africa and perhaps loosely scattered all the way over to Indonesia. He lacks only syntax to have the unique capacity for communal or group intelligence (if one guy is smart, the whole group is smarter—a premise, I believe, of business psychologists today, and of course requiring syntax). Getting from there to here seems like a daunting undertaking so let's go back to the baby steps. Perhaps you don't know syntax? It's essentially grammar, past, present, future, how to construct meaningful sentences.

Everyone—well, many people—are aware that the dinosaurs went extinct, except for the birds, 65 million years ago, because a large asteroid probably hit the earth down in the Gulf of Mexico, and the fallout did a number on the earth's climate, with volumes of poisonous gases in the air and certainly some severely altered temperatures due to all the dust and gases in the atmosphere. So why did the birds and mammals survive? Perhaps because they were warm blooded and had protective insulation (fur and feathers) but certainly because of some intrinsic feature that better fit them to the altered circumstance.

If one wishes to underscore such a scenario, they only have to look a little further back to the Permian extinction roughly 250 million years ago. Yes, there have been a number of periods in the past when God, in his wisdom, decided to reset the clock, but probably none so devastation as the Permian, in which possibly 90 percent of all existing life forms became extinct. What probably happened then was that the super continent of Pangea started to break up which "ignited" volcanic activity the like of which had not been seen for billions of years, since the Archaen. Back then, there was no life to get caught up in the gears. Whatever the theological transgressions of the fish, mollusks and amphibians of the Permian, they certainly paid for it with their lives, but not all the denizens of the deep did; the better adapted to the harsh new circumstances by sheer luck or perhaps the pure in heart, did survive, to probably considerably altered conditions, to then evolve into dinosaurs and mammals down the road. So, what is the lesson to be learned? Dare I venture to put forward the thesis that volcanism is bad for ya! The unholy trinity of gases—carbon monoxide, carbon dioxide, and sulphur dioxide—form corrosive compounds from carbonic to sulphuric acid that, if you get enough of it, will kill ya. I don't think that Al Gore may have gone that far.

Anyhow, vulcanism was not restricted to the Permian. What would happen if you had a lot of these noxious substances in the air but not enough to kill all of you? Well, I suspect, probably, that it would kill many of the "weak sisters," the old, the blind, and the lame.

But what would be the survival option under these circumstances? Well, Charlene, Margaret, and Dodi are out picking berries and digging up roots and Dodi says, "Bad smell," Margaret says, "Hurts my eyes and throat," and Dodi says, "Let's get out of here and find someplace where no smell"—syntax. While Don, David, and Uriah are out on the plains hunting antelope, Don says, "Bad smell." David says, "Me mighty hunter." Uriah says, "On, on, me find a way or make it"—no syntax. Who's going to survive? That scenario may have been repeated a thousand times over across the plains. Again, the powerful female's mitochondria favoured syntax against bull-headed stupidity, and the rest, as they say, is history (or evolution). One little unforeseen corollary: since more smart women may have survived, it may have generated beautiful females in competition for available males and the dumb males, sensing an evolutionary opportunity, threw familial responsibilities to the four winds to enjoy the cornucopia. The combined tribal wisdom (collective knowledge through syntax) would work to protect the more "with it" members, sort of like the reverse of smoking does today. It would probably not have gone to the extent of making gas masks out of sabre-toothed tiger skins but perhaps locating in a sheltered valley next to a lake that might absorb some of the more noxious gases and staying in the cave out of the acid rain. Sure, this is a bit of a spoof, but such behaviours as not smoking can give the proponents a big advantage in the long run. How much more might staying out of noxious volcanic gases have advantaged the syntactically equipped so long ago?

But what are we talking about? The coming of consciousness was some 50,000–100,000 years ago. There was no Pangea or asteroid problems then, as far as we know. But hold on there, sports fans. As depicted on the CBC's *The Passionate Eye* on June 16, 2010, there was a cataclysmic earth event 75,000 years ago, if the three scientists on the program are to be believed. There was a super volcano over in Sumatra connected to the same subduction zone that caused the big quake and tsunami of 2005. The scar is still visible in the 100-mile long lake—the huge volumes of noxious gases spewed out would have encircled the planet for perhaps decades. The geologist in the program only obliquely referred to the type of lava as rhyolite, but this stuff causes explosive volcanism. The ocean temperature appears to have dropped some 10 degrees Fahrenheit, suggesting that a mini ice age or at least an increase in the existing one had been set off. Ice cores from Greenland show large increases in CO_2 and SO_2 in the earth's atmosphere—enough of such poisonous vapours to dispatch a goodly number of those not equipped mentally or physically or vocally to survive. The odds on survivors? Those who could participate in syntactically-ridden collective wisdom—in other words, if we shelter ourselves now we may survive to fight another day. The scientists on the program estimated that the event could have taken the lives of half the population on the earth. For those to whom this may seem all a bit of a stretch, think back to the hole in the ozone layer and remember how that was handled. No debate, no questions like with global warming. Rather, we got a very simple equation: ozone = safety from the solar wind. On the other hand, no ozone would be analogous to standing on the core of a nuclear reactor when the cooling system broke down. So there was no argument. We had to fix it and fix it fast, or we could say good-bye to all non-aquatic species. This shows us we actually can act when we have to, through collective or accumulated knowledge, but don't leave the Chinese philosophers out of this: for every yin there is a yang, perhaps a flaw in the psyche or subconscious makeup of our stalwart survivors, such that they see themselves as demigods, too clever by half, to ever again be trapped by the simplistic machinations of this geologic process prone orb. How might God reward such pretentiousness?

The coming of consciousness, as depicted in the story of Adam and Eve is easily seen as many millennia before God gets ticked off with the perversity of his most advanced creation , but the story of the coming of consciousness was not invented by a bunch of bushwhacked hunter-gatherers. There was actually a pivotal event in our past history. One can only speculate about the required neural changes that took place; however, syntactical language appears to be the reason for the change, or the result. This causes us to question: Was the coming of language the cause or the effect of the great change? What happened to make a connection between the right and left brain to enable man to coordinate skill with intuition, thereby creating a smarter human being? And how was this great change, this coming of consciousness, ever discovered, let alone recorded as an event for posterity in the biblical narrative?

It is quite likely that before the coming of consciousness, before 75,000 years ago, that the new ape on the block (*Homo sapiens*) wasn't much more that that—a particularly smart ape. His linguistic abilities would doubtlessly have been better than just inflected grunts. He probably had names for things and could construct simple sentences such as "Man kill cat." Whatever the celestial magic that instituted syntax (grammar) it did not just change communication, it changed perception. "Suddenly" observed "things" needed explanations—the why of all that observed stuff. Cheeze! How do you explain a thunderstorm if your loin cloth is all wet? And why are you wearing a loin cloth? Explain that! Are your privates cold? And why are they private? Do you remember the explanation in the story of Adam and Eve of the embarrassment of nakedness? We don't just need structure in our sentences; we need structure in our lives, so we invent a multiplicity of gods to explain the unexplainable. But as we come out of the forests and off the plains into an organized society, most certainly the vengeance of hostile gods was very useful in maintaining an operable social organization.

> *"The fear of Hells the hangman's whip to hold the wretch in order."*
>
> —R. Burns

Most certainly the vengeance of hostile gods was very useful in designing a workable system. It was not until those pesky Hebrews came along with their monotheistic concepts that extraterrestrial prowess was removed from a simple policing role. Now it was up to you under the umbrella of a beneficent God (but smiting still remained an interim option). It's all very logical and congruent with what actually happened, but people continue to insist on some sort of Walt Disney magic. It doesn't need that; it's all perfectly rational and logical.

There remains the question of how an improved cerebral connection might have empowered those ancients so that they were able to solve simple problems. Unsaddled as they were with modern day stresses, they still had to solve problems that occurred in the level of their daily existence. In gross aspect, things haven't changed that much.

One would have to probe deeply into evolutionary theory to come up with explanations for some of the rapid changes that we know took place, but as the evolutionary pace quickens, we begin to see a definitive colliery emerge. This idea is seen in *A Brain for All Seasons*,[16] but it was first stated by Louis Leakey (the discoverer of all those early man artefacts in the Olduval gorge): "Domestication leads to very rapid evolutionary change." The idea here is that in a domestic environment, behavioural change can be very rapid and behavioural change is the antecedent of permanent biological change. Malcolm Gladwell, in *The Tipping Point*,[17] mentions an interesting possible corollary to Leakey's domestication thesis. He notes that the size of the brain seems to reflect the group size, as though one needed the extra brain capacity to deal with the additional requirements of having those additional people around. *Homo habalis* wandered the plains in core family groups, whereas *Homo erectus* was forced together into what was probably a much larger group, by the drought, wandering limited areas round the Rift Valley Lakes or staying close to the bays on the coast. The closely packed larger group would then require syntax to make one's intentions clear, and syntax required a more effective brain.

Again, it has been suggested that the domestication that took place occurred due to syntactic speech, which in turn would have affected the way the corpus colossi operated. This new innovation included the rules of grammar and the stringing of words into sentences to convey a meaningful message in past, present, or future tense. All from Mitochondrial Eve! (Did you ever wonder why females are so much better talkers than males?) Most of the gathering and all the nursing and raising of children and caretaking has been done by the women, evolving into a much more verbally rich environment

---

16 William H. Calvin, *A Brain for all Seasons: Human Evolution and Abrupt Climate Change* (Chicago: University of Chicago Press, 2002).
17 Malcolm Gladwell, *The Tipping Point* (New York: Little, Brown & Company, 2000).

than that of the solitary males stalking their prey. This proves to man that woman are just genetically better talkers! To reinforce that concept, we have the following little item as a meaningful romantic aside that most certainly would have involved syntax.

We don't know how far back love goes, but it has been suggested that Cupid was another gift to humanity by our Mitochondrial Eve. When one's species is depleted to within a few thousand souls, someone had better come up with a solution pretty quick, and what better way than in bed! We have always believed that love developed between male and female humans to fire up the defence of the reproduction process by having the male "fall in love" with the females so that he would stick around to protect her and their offspring from predators. However, a physical connection was never found until now.

Recent research on prairie voles (as reported in the science section of *The Economist*—early 2010) may have come close to the answer. These little rodents fall in love, for all intent and purpose, and stay monogamous. They live very domestic lives, thereby developing both a propagator and developer gene to produce the hormones required to lock in the lover, so to speak. If the genes are present in both male and female halves of the pair, a monogamous relationship occurs. If one or both of the genes is absent in either half, then no relationship is formed, and the search continues (Jezebel and the divorce gene?). Was this indeed another of the Mitochondrial Eve's gifts to humanity or just another way of conning the unaware male into a monogamous relationship? If it was "our Eve," was it the seafood diet that ultimately provided the protein to construct the gene, to provide the hormone to make one fall "in love"? Was this instinct passed on through the female human species to eat one's fish in order to ensure that love would enter our lives?

Scientists have used fluorescent substances from jellyfish in trying to distinguish "true love" from a "very well rehearsed con job." Apparently, it works. To date, no one has attempted to correlate the divorce rate with the switch from herring and potatoes to fast food, but as an aside, when looking for love, I suggest you ask if your love interest is a seafood fancier as well.

The Australian Aborigines were truly the Christopher Columbus of their day. The land they eventually settled in was almost as arid as the one they left behind, but perhaps the easy trapping of koalas and kangaroos offered a welcome respite to sabre-toothed tigers. The "dream time" legends of the Aborigines may provide a further insight into this nomadic time. There are some very ancient remains in Palestine, which have not been placed in any specific migration but some of the "droppings off" of the great trek eastward. However, no one has advanced such a theory, and there is no immediate significant evidence for doing so. Besides, the migration is believed to have crossed the Red Sea at Aden and the Persian Gulf at the Strait of Harmuz.

The most intriguing, and possibly the most significant, alleged ancient item found is in the vicinity of Timbuktu, in the very arid Sahara Desert, proving that not all the migrations were eastward. The ancient Sahara was not always the desert it is today. Five thousand years ago there were elephants and hippopotami drinking from the now dry rivers. To explain such a curious reversal of fortune we need to look to astronomy and meteorology. When the earth is closest to the sun in summer rather than in winter, because of the off-centre elliptical orbit, the heat at the Tropic of Cancer is roughly 10 percent greater than normal (from *A Brain for All Seasons*).[18] This is sufficient to create horrendous vertical convection currents, which draw moist air into the desert from the Atlantic and Mediterranean, which gets blasted vertically by the rising hot air and then subsequently cools at roughly 4°F/1,000 feet of elevation. The water vapour condenses into humungous thunderheads, which dump buckets of rain on the parched earth, which in turn grows vegetation, which attracts herbivores, which attracts carnivores (including man). The earth continues its orbital cycle, which stops the above noted rain and vegetation. This causes the great migration to cease and everyone goes back to whence they came. Timbuktu is situated on the Niger River in the Sahara just 6 or 7 degrees south of the Tropic of Cancer. It is possible that it enjoyed both direct sunlight and water and became an excellent spot for a tall African group to congregate and settle. Carved in the rocks in the vicinity of Timbuktu are alleged to be

18 William H. Calvin, *A Brain for all Seasons*.

astronomical symbols. Sirius—the Dog Star—is alleged to be depicted as a double star, which it is, and Jupiter is shown with four moons, which it has. These depictions—being thousands of years old—are correct, and today we only see the actual items through binoculars or telescopes. The local legends of probably the Dogon tribe of West Africa tell of "little blue men" having done the pictographs, which causes one to think of the Welsh and the blue vegetable dye (Wode) that they smeared on their skin to protect themselves from the elements and enemy's swords. Perhaps the early Saharan clans were "proto-Welch" and migrated north due to climate change, leaving their technical and astronomical expertise in the desert behind to eke out an existence in a strange and not so friendly land. There is no estimate of when the rock carvings were completed, as far as I know, but the implication is they were very ancient and drawn by someone who was knowledgeable in astronomy.

So there is a nebulous little item that interjects here, on which a number of people have speculated. What it amounts to is that there appears to have been an advanced civilization somewhere prior to the ice melting. All the flood stories sort of superseded and obliterated the memory of all that had gone before, except for that persistent legend of a "lost continent." The "loose ends and free floaters" have given rise to much fanciful speculation but it is a little difficult to deny some of the specifics. Hancock in *Fingerprints of the Gods*[19] does a fairly convincing job of proving that the Great Pyramids of Giza were not built by the Pharaohs but were constructed long before and the pharaohs just appropriated them at a later time. Part of his argument centres on the Olmecs of Central America, whose carved heads unmistakably demonstrate negroid features suggesting an African connection. All that I will say is that there appears to be a missing chapter here somewhere.

The idea of the pyramids predating the pharaohs is partly at least based on the three pyramids of Giza being an earthly representation of the three stars in Orion's Belt and how they would have appeared two thousand years before Pharonic Egypt even evolved. That of course brings in the idea of the twelve houses of the zodiac and the

19 Graham Hancock, *Fingerprints of the Gods: The Evidence of Earth's Last Civilizations* (New York: Three Rivers Press, 1995).

mysterious idea of the number base of twelve and where it might have originated as well as all of the resultant geometric and time stuff (360 degrees is a circle, 24 hours in a day).

If there ever were the 'little blue guys' at Timbuktu they were superseded by a tall group of Africans.

Here they are (the big guys who came after the little blue guys) standing on the north shore of Africa, watching a herd of élan that they were pursuing strike out for the Gibraltar shore in order to escape the hunters' spears. Gibraltar is directly north of Timbuktu. The strait was not as wide then as it is today, because to build those mile-thick northern glaciers required a lot of water, and sea level had dropped 300 to 400 feet. The strait may have been less than 10 km, or five miles wide, making it a quite easily accessible escape route for the élan. These people, being smarter than one might expect, realized they needed a craft to fjord the strait, and after constructing a boat of sorts, they set out for the other side. At that time it was not much of a junket compared to what their Australians counterparts had to contend with. With the level of the Mediterranean down 300 to 400 feet, they had only to negotiate the strait and were then treated to broad vistas of gently rolling meadows on the exposed continental shelf of what is now Spain and France. They hurriedly returned to their home across the water and held a council meeting that very night to describe the veritable Garden of Eden just across the way. The vote went strongly for an immediate move to the land of milk and honey—no more dust storms, no more blisters—and in retrospect, fifty thousand years before the Moors would do it all again (though no continental shelf in the latter move).

The appearance of Cro-Magnon man about this time would almost fit the picture, and perhaps in that very area as well! Did Cro-Magnons become the Amorites after a little adjustment? And were they originally Negroid? They (the Amorites) were tall people, and a biblical reference ("There were giants living in those days") could be referencing the Cro-Magnons. The Cro-Magnons and Amorites were both tall people, could they have been one and the same? The Bible does not seem to be a time specific document, with the tales being handed down via word of mouth, generation to generation. How many generations does it actually cover? (How long do we have to wait for National Geographic to do the gene study?) So far, the most basic gene seems to be from central Asia. It is not yet clear how that gene may have entered Europe, but it did so way before the Mongol invasion, which means there must have been an earlier shortcut. There is not much documentation yet on the groups that don't physically or linguistically fit the mould, such as the Basques and the Finns.

In my version, the migration from Timbuktu proved to be a wise decision for the nomads. The streams were full of fish and the fertile "shelf" plain saw the beginnings of agriculture as the nomads settled into a stable social organization. Remember, they now had syntax, and syntax makes collective intelligence and information accumulation possible. It is possible that small settlements with permanent dwellings were constructed. These people had evolved into a more intelligent being than their forefathers (just remember, this is all speculation). And there is another speculative item: if these shelf dwellers did indeed start agriculture, plant food contains very little vitamin D, so their sojourn on the shelf would have sped up the whitening out process, which is perhaps what we are seeing with the blond Amorites sometime later.

Many may contest my version of the point of entry of the Africans into Europe, as most archaeologists appear to believe that they took the long way around, through the Levant, Anatolia, Bosporus, et al. Recently, though, that interpretation has been called into question as a result of a perceived nineteenth and early twentieth century racial bias, to whit: African culture could not possibly have been responsible for the beautiful art work in the caves of Spain and France. Similar suspicion is also directed toward many of the carvings, the most obvious of the latter being the big bellied, big breasted, big buttoxed Venuses found scattered across Europe.

It is the contention of some, that the Venuses are a depiction of the generic aberration called Steatopygia. Apparently, the mutation was fairly common amongst the Bushmen and Pygmies and was highly valued as a fetal survival feature within those very ancient genetic lines. It is suspected of having had something to do with protecting the fetus in very hot latitudes, so this became a desirable feature, even a beauty approbation, in short, a venus. Of course, much of this is probably just conjecture, but for the archaeologists to say nothing about it renders their conclusion, or lack of one, suspect. They look negroid to me. So I'm hanging in there with the proposal of a major African migration into south Western Europe via the Straits of Gibraltar, sometime after the coming of consciousness, perhaps fifty thousand years ago.

The National Geographic says that something happened about seventy thousand years ago, perhaps in response to the terrible climactic conditions, or perhaps in reaction to that super volcano over in Sumatra, or both. The Geographic also mentions the ambivalent nature of the Sahara, how herbivores might move in when it was lush and leave again when it dried out. They also show a migration along the southern shore of the Mediterranean. Although I originally went with a migration north from Timbuktu, I could live with their migration route as long as they are allowed to cross the Strait of Gibraltar. There is apparently some evidence for a migration back across that strait some millennia later, perhaps as pressure built from the migrating groups from Asia.

As long as we are speculatively polishing up our fair-play image by washing out any hint of racial prejudice, I should like to present a sore spot of mine. We know that *Homo sapiens* and *Homo neanderthalensis* co-existed on the plains of Europe for quite some time. When the Neanderthals finally exited this earthly coil, the assumption is made that we did it, that we are guilty of genocide against our cousins. One might justifiably question if this is just a reflection of our own awareness of what a rape and pillage monster we have become as a result of civilization. I'm not suggesting that we were ever a bunch of goodie two shoes, but in all probability our depredations on our genetic cousins has been overstated. After all, our 1 to 4 percent Neanderthal genes suggest that our relationship was more one of love than war.

Yes, the circumstantial evidence for the extinction of the large herbivores is difficult to duck, but extending the idea to our relatives is a bit of overreach, particularly when I have a perfectly logical and plausible explanation, so let's just aim for half a loaf. "Honest, Officer, we did kill the big guys to feed the family, but we never laid a hand on our cousins." Actually, even that's not true. Sure we did develop some pretty smart hunting strategies but the massive number of huge beasts all smashed together in great piles of bones says that a large part of the story is untold. We know that it all happened in a very short period (less than 1,000 years between 13,000 and 12,000 years). We may have been good hunters, but we were not that good—something else happened (see Chapter 4, "Geology").

Before I present the case for Neanderthal "love not war," I should like to partially clear our reputation as Neolithic species exterminators. The case against us for killing off much of the ice age wildlife is based mainly on the juxtaposition in time of that extinction and the appearance of the Clovis Point a particularly lethal, finely crafted spear point. I'm not saying that we weren't involved at all—we obviously were—but we were not wholly responsible.

Recent investigations by geologists in Nova Scotia suggest that there may have been a particularly large meteor impact about this time, and in somewhat the same manner as the impact that killed the dinosaurs at the end of the Cretaceous, this one may have done in the large ice age mammals. But there is an even further dimension to this suggestion. We (geologists) have long considered this ice age extinction as having been connected to a reversal of the polarity of the earth. This phenomenon happens periodically, and we don't really know why, but meteor impact is about as good a theory as any. There is another theory about the shifting of the entire crust of the earth (see Chapter 4, "Geology").

The fact that there may (must) have been such a pole reversal is attested to by the discovery in northern Canada of a mastodon struck down in the act of chewing buttercups and subsequently becoming frozen in the ice. So why would pole reversal cause such devastation? Well, the earth's magnetism forms a shield around us to divert the solar wind of charged particles. We can see this diversion in the form of the northern lights, which shows these little charged hellions being diverted and their energy dissipated by spiralling into the atmosphere. When the poles reverse, will there be time? Seconds? Minutes? Hours? Days? Wherein we have no protection from the solar wind, except perhaps that provided by the ozone layer. So anyone standing out of doors will get zapped by these high energy particles, which if they don't kill you outright will play havoc with your reproductive system. Humans living in caves and other types of shelter, including those living further south, will have largely survived the onslaught. Of course, we have no reading on how many of our ancestors may have perished along with the sabre-toothed tigers, but God never promised that there would never be some collateral damage. In all probability, the weakened surviving mammals would have been easier prey for the Neolithic *Homo sapiens*, with their advanced weapons and syntactical hunting strategies. There is no need to suppose that we killed our cousins. It's just that the best-equipped species won the survival game. Apparently, the last pole reversal has been dated at some 780,000 years ago, so it is likely that we can't use that excuse to duck the demise of the big guys. There seems to be something wrong with that dating, though, because of the buttercup mastodon. Let's see what the Maritimers can do with the meteor impact and of course there are several other explanations. Why did I bring it up? Just thought you might be interested.

It's a bit of a convoluted tale, perhaps, but we raconteurs have never been known to be brief. It goes with the territory, so stoke up the fire and prepare for a tale of derring-do. Back in the 1950s, the Canadian mining industry was simply exploding, with new fortunes being made daily. I was a rosy-faced youth with a brand new degree in economic geology. My darling old professor got me a job with the American Smelting and Refining outfit in Buchans, Newfoundland. At the time, they owned one of the more lucrative base metal mines in the business, in central Newfoundland. The company tended to operate somewhat like a feudal barony (they were alleged to have refused to transport Joey Smallwood, "the only living father of Confederation," on their railway). He was a Liberal, and my view of the company was somewhere to the right of Attila the Hun. They "owned" the centre of Newfoundland. I only tell you this to illustrate a later point.

During the 1930s depression, the Newfoundlanders had shot every moose in the province. As a result the wolves all died too. So when moose were subsequently reintroduced they had no enemies and the population exploded. There was hardly a tree branch below 10 feet in the whole province. So when we loaded up the tractor train to take us out onto the bogs of central Newfoundland, we loaded on cases of canned goods, a couple of cases of dynamite, a 30-30 carbine, and a case of ammunition. Do I have to spell it out for you? It was like, go live off the land. Tractor trains for resupply are expensive.

Well, one night as we sat around the fire yarning (no TV), I exclaimed to my French Canadian bushman that I could not understand how ancient man was ever able to kill those huge ice age mammals, let alone the mastodons. Just be aware that this smart-assed university punk had previously made fun of Richards old single-shot 30-30. He responded quite calmly, "Tomorrow, I show you."

Moose were everywhere. We hurled sticks of dynamite at them to keep them out of the stream from whence we drew our water. The next morning, my chore in this little illustrative exercise was to walk across the tundra rustling a paper bag to distract the moose while Richard circled around behind the moose and shot him through the diaphragm with a single shot. That huge animal just lay down and died, unable to breathe. In Richard's immortal words, "That's how." It's only now that I can really appreciate the ancient hunters. They developed that hunting strategy because they had syntax and could plot a strategy, instead of just taking on a mammoth head on. And of course, they had developed the spear-thrower to the same advantage, which the Neanderthals didn't have.

Apparently, the Neanderthals voice box was not so ideally located as that of *Homo sapien*. They probably never could accomplish syntactical speech. No syntax, no groupthink strategies. This conclusion is attested to by the mangled corpses in Neanderthal graves. So probably don't take on a mastodon head-on! Coming up behind a large animal distracted by your hunting buddy and launching a spear at its diaphragm from a relatively safe distance— "that's how." And moose tenderloin is good for developing brain cells, not as good as fish, perhaps, but right up there—and most certainly good for a myriad of hunting tales (which is good for male bonding). And it was in all probability only the Neanderthal widows that lent us their genes, but we didn't speak the same language, so don't get smart about us guys taking advantage of the little cave girls. Besides, those Neanderthal guys were really big mothers.

Seriously though, hunting tactics would have been the equivalent of today's military strategies, and although it may seem such a minor technical or strategic advance to us today, that attitude on our part starkly outlines how little we appreciate the coming of consciousness and the very shallow learning curve as *Homo sapiens* gradually learned how to put two and two together with the help of his hunting buddies until he was able to vanquish those ice age monsters. So, without that conscious communicative ability, the Neanderthals' fortunes waned on the post glacial plains of Europe, while his cousins became more dexterous and proficient and simply out-hunted him. In the process, of course, we killed off many of the large mammals of the Ice Age, or at least those that were left after the meteor impact, but there is bound to be some collateral damage from advanced technology! The Neanderthals were simply the victims of superior thought processes, not any ill intent on our part.

I do recognize that to use such gruesome hunting techniques today would probably get one drummed out of the human race. Standing off 300 yards with a high-powered rifle with Weaver scope somehow appears more humane.

End of a lengthy and exciting era for men. Now we are just going to have to be smart like the women—damn!

Then it happened—between 18,000 and 12,000 years the ice melted, the sea level rose, and the settled nomads on the shelves of France and Spain were flooded out. They were on the move again, but not back to Africa. When the ice melted, the plains of Europe became a vast sea of grassland supporting huge herds of herbivores, and our adventurers became hunter/gatherers again. The event is perhaps recorded in the caves of Lascoux in France and other venues in the Pyrenees. Those cave paintings ceased around 13,500 years ago as the boys moved north—again! But as always when one tried to account for everything, there will be part of the chapter missing. We have always thought in terms of hunter-gatherers. What about the fishers? They aren't going to move inland! Where did they "go"? Across the Atlantic?

Again, most of the ice would have been melted off the plains of Europe by this time so that the ice age mammals no longer had to migrate so far south and the rise of water in the Mediterranean would have flooded out the settlements on the shelves of southern France and northeastern Spain. So the residents moved north with the animals, and then some got waylaid by the Danube River and migrated east/southeast to the Black Sea.

Again perhaps the point of entry of my version of the oral tradition is slightly off, as most archaeologists believe that the Africans took the long way around. But, according to me, these Negroid people were moving north directly. Edouard Piette in1867 interpreted some of the female sculptures at Brassempony and Grimaldi as African. Subsequently doubt has been cast on that interpretation, but I'm going with Piette (p54 *Prehistoric Art*—Randall White) (See page 32 for early archaeological racial prejudice.).[20]

With a difference in diet—grains have little vitamin D—and less sunlight, our intrepid wanderers more than likely suffered from a vitamin deficiency, especially vitamin D. The evolutionary answer would have been to "bleach" out.

Sometime in their wanderings, the group that reached the west end of the Black Sea appears to have done just that. We have documentation of tall blond people known to history as the Amorites in the general area of the Black Sea. Also, Hammurabi of Babylonian fame is alleged to have been an Amorite. But who they were and what happened to them is anybody's guess. The Finns are tall and blond and speak a language that has no known roots, and the Amorites would have followed the game north, would they not? Ian Morris says that there were still quite a few of them around by 1200 BC to get caught up in the upheavals of those times.[21]

Others of the displaced persons continued on north into what is today Germany, and here we can come up with a somewhat less speculative speculation. When we sagely nod agreement to the idea of black Africans "bleaching out," we tend to see it as a general overall fading of skin pigment, but that completely ignores when it didn't happen that way. My antecedents on my fraternal grandmother's side were Germans, and they carried a gene for what was called

20 Randall White, *Prehistoric Art: The Symbolic Journey of Humankind* (New York: Harry N. Abrams, Inc. Publishers, 2003), 32.
21 Morris, *Why the West Rules*.

"Hennigar hair." Their hair is often reddish and tightly curled (tousled), like that of Africans. And if you have ever observed a dark haired person bleach their hair, you will be aware that it will often go through a stage where it is red. Not only that, but the bleaching out of the skin pigment is frequently intermittent rather than a general body wide fading out (i.e., freckles). The Hennigars had tight curly, red hair, and freckles. Perhaps latitude had something to do with different processes and the colour of the Amorites, or perhaps they may have been significantly genetically different to begin with. Or perhaps, for whatever reason, they underwent different processes to cope with the threat of low vitamin D levels. Michael Jackson laid claim to a somewhat rare autoimmune condition involving the body's defence mechanism attacking the skin pigment cells. It is called vitiligo, and why should one not consider that, if the children of Scottish coal miners developed an autoimmune condition that kept them alive well into breeding age but killed them soon after menopause? The good Lord works in mysterious ways!

Of course it is just guessing without the genetic backup, but if Norwegians followed the game north to the west and Finns (Amorites) did the same thing to the east, wouldn't the interface produce an intermediate group like the Swedes? And shouldn't the gene project show that? For heaven's sake, don't believe this little imaginative scenario, but do follow the National Geographic's genetic project to establish origins and relationships.

There is always an antecedent to everything that we observe. Just because we don't see it or can't admit it doesn't mean that it isn't there. (See the item on "love.") To remain in our "comfort zones" we would very much like to say, "It is now and always has been." No it hasn't! "The old order changeth to the new!" and just because you may have your feet firmly stuck in the clay of time does not mean that it did not happen otherwise. My interpretations may be a little unorthodox, so please get out there and prove me wrong!

Because of the advanced evolutionary changes instigated in humans by the vicissitudes of glacially instituted climate changes over 2.5 million years, "natural selection" has largely become decoupled from human evolution. Put another way, the reason for the decoupling is that we are now smart enough that we have pretty

[51]

well figured out the sabre-toothed tiger and drought things, and we know enough to get out of the way of the juggernaut when the going gets tough—I think! So because of that great innovation of syntax, which allowed collective knowledge, we have accumulated enough know-how to take the required action to avoid any more bottlenecks. However, as fate might have it, this time perhaps we will have to stand and deliver rather than migrate. Looks like a losing game plan if we follow the advice of our politicians. Perhaps conventional wisdom, corruption, and empire building may succeed where natural selection left off. But if we don't get it figured out right and in time, we can be dispatched forthwith, to join the great Auk and the Dodo bird.

Just a bit of caution here for those who would like to believe that we have actually outgrown and outdistanced all of that very stressful environmental evolutionary stuff. I would suggest that perhaps we are just entering a new phase of evolutionary change where the fittest are not just the physically fittest but are also mentally adjusted to the new electronic milieu. I would caution that how we relate to our environment is not centered on the natural world but the electronic world that we have created. It is about to raise its ugly head, and not necessarily favouring us old guys.

We no longer confront sabre-toothed tigers with spears, but we do confront climate change with computers. Barring complexity, what's the difference? They are both trying to kill us. Psychologists tell us that they can already detect changes in our neural functioning as well as in our neural configuration. What they are suggesting is that physical evolution may have been mitigated by our modern lifestyle advancements (perhaps not if obesity is considered) but look out nerve central—*bon chance, mon ami*!

Back to good ol' solid science type stuff.

Scientists have always marvelled at the narrow, delicate balance of temperature on the earth. The planet's distance from the sun and its inclination toward or away from the sun is sufficient to keep water mostly in a liquid state and promote the seasons. When the basic plan gets a little out of whack, we get major changes in climate and season, as well as some major changes in life forms or habits. Those of a religious persuasion have always said, "Well, thank God for the Creator's mindful tending of the store."

Understanding the intricate detail of how it all comes about is a very recent phenomenon, but perhaps no less miraculous. Is it really all part of a grand plan, or is it just a statistical aberration? For instance, there were glaciations on the planet long before life appeared. Were they trial runs? Has man's immense ego twisted perfectly ordinary celestial processes in order to highlight his/ her existence as out of the ordinary, something that requires an omnipotent being to look after our special interests?

It probably doesn't matter much in the grand celestial scheme of things. Life forms come and go. Stars have life cycles too, and ours will eventually gobble us up, but probably not before our particular species has gone through some unimaginable changes and/or disappeared altogether. "A thousand ages in thy sight are like an evening gone." All bets are off as to how long our tenure may last. Some forms of coral and clam like animals have made it 300 to 400 million years, but the more complex the life form, the shorter seems to be its lifespan—at least up until now. Remember, our particular strain of mammalian evolution has only been around for a few tens of millions of years, and we have only come into our own once the dinosaur exited stage right—65 million years ago. In response, we moved up the food chain. In the meantime, whatever the origin of this big brain, it's probably well past the time when we should have begun using it in our own interest instead of adopting the role the dinosaur used to play to keep us mammals in check. Do you suppose they were clairvoyant and knew that there had to be some sort of external intervention?

One item along the way to our ultimate destiny—whatever that may prove to be—might be to understand our own history. And that, essentially, is what this little literary exercise is aimed toward.

Our big brain, in which we put such stock, has not always been an unmitigated blessing. The planet is a pretty scary place for a naked ape to be wandering around without a gun. With the coming of consciousness, we began to understand just how scary the world is. St. Augustine and others crafted a beautiful narrative in the grand style of the oral tradition so we could understand and be reassured of man's place on the earth and in space and time, with all of the other denizens, the whole caboodle overseen by an omnipotent being who will look after our interests as long as we behave—sort of quid pro quo. (Well, you don't see any sabre-toothed tigers around, do you?) I think that we were also admonished to not get too full of ourselves. Not an easy prescription when handed this awesome biological computer atop our shoulders. Our scientific successes are mind boggling—in the social realm, perhaps not so much. A little tuning up along the lines that the good saint prescribed might be in order.

This latter reference is intended to draw attention to the role that narrative has played in our upward struggle. If perhaps some items got slightly skewed, it all helps to make the story come out right. We shall see—or perhaps not!

I admit I was wrong about the initial premise of the in phase/ out of phase light technique going to identify rocky planets around other stars. It didn't work very well, I guess, but the tiny differences in a star's luminosity as a planet traverses its disc has worked, and those dogged guys have identified something like a thousand planets around other stars. Most are of course gaseous giants like Jupiter, but some of the tinier ones are probably rocky. One may wonder what evil lurks on which of those sister planets.

So you see, even I am vulnerable to error, so don't be shy— criticize! If nothing else, you might stumble on something new or different or perhaps put some of the scientists on the spot.

All of this may appear maudlin in concept, but then our survival might just depend on an approach of questioning wonder. One of the detriments to our scheme for survival seems to be an innate inability to see what is staring us right in the face. However, psychologists caution against being too hard on our scepticism. They tell us that distrust of glib explanations has helped keep the number of "snake oil salesmen" at a reasonable level, at least until recently. In addition, most of us have been able to avoid "the grape drink"—the flames and gunfire of the false messiahs. But our defences have been much better than our insights. Perhaps seeing glaciation as the handmaiden of God may help us to select the high road. And, oh yes! Blame love on glaciation, *mon cherie*.

But where does all this leave us, and why have we wasted so much time with all that ancillary stuff resulting from glaciation? Well, my darling, don't get into questioning God's methods; you're not that smart. We are the result of an over 2-million-year process that we don't really completely understand. The arrow of progress was obviously positive, and though many of us would like to instruct God on how He might have better done things, He's God. So button up your lip! Let us glory in amazement at how it has all worked out. Oh, sure, many people perished on the way, but there never was a written guarantee of longevity. Besides, how else are you going to get rid of the also rans? God sort of seems to know what He is doing, even though it might elude us. Somewhere, someplace, there is an admonition about not questioning the Almighty's methods. So, okay, I'm a geologist, and I think glaciation is sacred, while you may have a somewhat different perspective. That does not mean that either one of us is wrong, just that our particular perspective may not take everything into account. I happen to be awed by God's great glaciation and I am perfectly willing to doff my hat to the Almighty's approach to doing things. You may wish to argue? So let's hear it. The celestial implication of glaciation may be in question but certainly not the result. If I were writing a play, that would certainly be the sequence.

CHAPTER 4: GEOLOGY

SKIP THIS CHAPTER AT your peril, because herein is explained why some of the terrible things that happened to our forefathers happened. Without this masterful interpretation of earth mechanics, one might be inclined to just gloss over the importance of events or the interpretation of the dynamics of mother earth to the point of dismissal, and that would defeat the whole enterprise. The objective is to explain not just what happened but how and why it happened and perchance to illustrate how God may work in such mysterious ways.

We will attempt to stay as far away from technical jargon as possible, but there are four terms that cannot be avoided, so let's take the bit in our teeth at the start and learn four very fundamental terms:

1. **Continental plate (or just plate)**. A large portion of the earth's surface (a continent) made up of rocks that are lighter than those that make up the ocean floor. These rocks are mostly sediments, such as sandstone and limestone, or altered sediments (metamorphics), such as marble, dolomite, quartzite, and schist/gneiss. The plate is sort of like an iceberg floating in the ocean, only it is rock floating in the earth's semi-fluid mantle underneath (refer to sectional of the earth).

2. **Faulting**. A crack in the earth where one side moves up and the other down. The whole incident accompanied by a large earthquake.

3. **Subduction (sliding under).** One great humungous slug of rock, part of the continent or even the ocean floor, slip/slides underneath another. Perhaps the best example is the sea floor off of the West Coast of BC and Washington State, where the ocean floor is sliding underneath the continent as the landmass floats inexorably westward. This process gives rise to the volcanoes south of the border and the earthquakes just off the coasts. There is an awful lot more to it, but only geologists need to know.

4. **Isostatic rebound.** Very simply, when those huge glaciers built up on the surface of the earth (the crust), they were very heavy. So heavy, in fact, that they pushed the solid crust of the earth down into the fluid mantle. When the ice melted, the crust rebounded to its former level—probably not all at once, like a jack-in-the-box, but slowly and haltingly over time. The number of levels of "raised beaches" up on the coast of Labrador suggest several millennia, as does the Younger Dryas (cold snap) several millennia after the rest of the ice had melted. We'll talk about this event later.

Way, way back, hundreds of millions of years ago, all of the dry land was jammed together into a supercontinent called Pangea (see verses 1:9 and 1:10 Genesis.) That biblical reference was not Pangea, although it was likely a precursor, which may have happened a number of times. Then, some 200 to 250 million years ago (mya), the convection currents within the plastic mantle (that layer just below the solid crust), for whatever reason, got under the super continent and began to break it up. North and South America were dispatched westward, rafting up the Rocky Mountains and the Andes on the leading edge of this immense bulldozer blade, as it relentlessly trudged westward at about the rate that your fingernails grow. Africa slammed into Europe, pushing up the Alps and a variety of other ranges all along the Adriatic over to Lebanon. At a different time, India plowed into Asia, creating the Himalayas. Sure, it was a little more complicated than that, but we don't need to joust with the devil in the details. Most people have heard some version of this continental drift theory (fact!). What may be new for many is the downwarping of portions of the crust attendant to the horizontal vector of this big push. Try it with a piece of paper. Sometimes it will pop up (mountains) and sometimes slumpdown (trough or downwarp). In practice, on the scale of continents, it sort of does both. Canadians will recognize the straits of Georgia/Queen Charlotte/Hecate Strait on the West Coast with islands upthrown to the west and mountains to the east. For Europe and Africa, it is the Mediterranean Sea, with the Alps to the north and the Atlas mountains to the south. Just a bit different for the Black Sea: downwarp to the north and the Anatolia Mountains (Turkey) to the south. For the Caspian Sea, the Caucasus mountains of Georgia and Armenia to the south and west and the Albany mountains to the south in Iran. There is even a large basin north of the Himalaya in Turkistan, once the site of a large lake, long since gone dry. So yes, dear reader, the Black Sea is exactly where it should be, geologically speaking, and no big adjustments are necessary. The big question is why God in his wisdom chose that venue to do such a number on so many of the planet's hapless denizens, who were just beginning to emerge from their small stone age hunter-gatherer groups—because they were a handy source of settlers for other areas?

We, of course, got lucky, because those pesky Hebrews seem to have had better raconteurs than anyone else, so all of the exigencies of their various treks conspired to give us a peek at what happened, albeit their take on it. In their version of the flood, the Hebrew God, Yahweh (actually not Yahweh yet, not even EL, but whatever the name used, the same God) got upset with their sinful ways and moved to put an end to all that. In the southern version, man had just become too noisy and had to be shut up.

Personally, I'm more attuned to the Hebrew version, but of course, I'm the recipient of their not-so-forgiving code. But this is supposed to be a geological treatise, not a sermon on morality. Suffice it to say that the Black Sea was sort of the recipient of a double-whammy, a down warp in front of the northeast corner of the African plate and the full frontal assault of the Arabian plate (see tectonic map for the subduction zone faults in the eastern Mediterranean, Persian Gulf, and Gulf of Oman). "Mercy, Noah, let's get outta there!" Because whenever you get these big continental plates crashing into each other (interfacing), you tend to get mountains building with very active earthquake zones. The San Andreas Fault in California is perhaps the most familiar to most listeners, and there the plates are just sliding past each other. In Turkey, it's more of a head-on deal. The North Anatolia fault just south of the Black Sea killed thousands in the earthquake of the 1990s, and it is just the result of the big subduction. If people would only listen to their resident geologist instead of treating him like a geek, just think of how many lives might be saved. Of course, geologists are somewhat more partial to explaining things after they happen than getting into the clairvoyance game. Time, as they say, marches on and waits for no one. So probably don't wait for the geologists. It's been about 7,500 years for poor ol' Noah and his beautiful blond bride.

Since we are finding God's wisdom a trifle perplexing in this emerging venue for the ascent of civilization, perhaps we might be permitted a tiny bit of really far-out speculation. I, for one, have always wondered why the holy city of Mecca is where it is. Friends say, "Well, pick a spot!" The Moslems go a bit further than that. I'm unsure of the correct detail, but I believe that they say that Abraham was down here. I don't think that he is thought to have had much to do with establishing the city, but he certainly would have lent the environs some sanctity. But then, the question arises, why did the old patriarch travel so far south when the Promised Land was supposed to be in Palestine? Perhaps it only became the Promised Land after Abraham's scouting mission. There is another curiosity of astronomical proportions that seems to point to this being a holy spot from way back.

Actually, three plates come together at the mouth of the Red Sea—The Afar Triple Junction, if you look at the tectonics. But you will notice on the map that the Jabal Turwaig and Bllyadh/Arma platerau in the centre of the Arabian peninsula look for all the world like there had been a giant asteroid impact, complete with a central rebound, an "astrobleme," meaning we aren't entirely sure what it is. Such an astronomical collision could surely have been instrumental in breaking the Arabian plate off of the African one, and perhaps even initiating the subduction to the northeast, rather than just continuing the parent plates' trip directly north, which might also account for the sea floor spreading in the Gulf of Aden. Not only that, but the fault that offsets the Red sea about halfway up almost exactly bisects the apparent impact feature. Now, hold on to your hat. If one takes the Arc of Subai as the centre of impact, then the fault passes right through Mecca. God promised no more floods, and having melted most of the glaciers, we can surely believe that He meant what He said, but He never mentioned anything about asteroids or big earthquakes on major faults. Perhaps unwittingly, or by design, that is why Mecca is such a holy place. Whether or not the ancients knew of the impact, they knew the place was special.

There is yet another feature: the big fault appears to be responsible for the fifth cataract on the Nile R. and if the asteroid/ fault/cataract had been a long, long time ago, the "waterfall" would have migrated much further up river.

So is a holy place just a holy place, or is there more to it than that? Was the Geological Survey of Canada over there in the Neolithic to advise the Stone Age inhabitants, and were they wearing blue coveralls? And what was their advice (that this was a very special, holy place, and the local denizens should regard it with great awe and reverence)?

Oh! All right, stop rapping my knuckles. I thought that I could avoid this, but apparently not, and I have it on the best authority: *The Biblical World*, by Isbouts (National Geographic).[22] So Abraham probably did go down there, not for God-instituted direction but because his concubine, Hagar, fled down there to avoid the punitive pressures being exerted by Abraham's wife, Sarah. Hagar, in order to keep body and soul together, took the southern rout with their (illigimate?) kid Ishmial in tow, and presumably ol' Abe went along because he didn't know what else to do (sound familiar, guys?). It does seem to be a bit peculiar, though, because apparently Sarah was a stunner, so much so that even the Pharaoh had the hots for her and Abe passed her off as his sister. I think that there is a word for that—should we call it "shilling" or use the other word? Oh, but

---

22 Jean-Pierre Isbouts, *The Biblical World: An Illustrated Bible* (Toronto: National Geographic Society, 2007).

"what a tangled web we weave once we practice to deceive". Ol' Abe parlayed the Pharaoh's infatuation with his beautiful wife into becoming a very rich man but eventually got "hoisted on his own petard". Apparently Sarah was at least temporarily sterile, and poor ol' Abe needed an heir (how ya going to be a patriarch without progeny), so he started playing around. Well, you know where that gets you. But that's good solid male reasoning. Apparently Sarah didn't see it quite that way, so what's a patriarch to do? Well, apparently Hagar wasn't about to put up with Sarah's coming down on her so decided to flee. But darling soul, she was not your average outdoors girl, so without really realizing what she was getting into, Hagar fled into the southern desert to avoid the wrath of Sarah. *Mon ami* Perrault, not a smart move! But apparently Abe followed her, because of his investment in the heir to be, mercy! Out of the frying pan into the fire, so to speak. Just about when Hagar is about to expire from dehydration, she stumbles on this beautiful spring of fresh water—you guessed it, saved by the beneficence of a benevolent God. Whatever, but Hagar gave Yahweh all of the credit, so she dedicated her son's life to the service of God and Ismael grew up to establish one of the world's great religions, the Moslem faith, and the spring that had saved them became Mecca.

So get ye to the library and read up on this exciting tale. But here we are descending from the high-minded echelon of faith to the not-so-high-minded geologist in the pub. But really we do need to find that itinerant soul to tell us that Hagar's spring is on the fault that splits the Red Sea in two because of the asteroid impact—and that spring is Mecca. The good Lord does indeed work in mysterious ways. But starting a whole new religion on the basis of a spring of fresh water does seem like a bit of a stretch, particularly to slake the thirst of one whom many might question the nature of her morality. It is perhaps a leap of faith. But I'm going with Hagar. This was indeed something of a miracle, and although I'm a bit tenuous about establishing a whole new religion on such a flimsy basis, who am I to question the wisdom of Yahweh?

But darling Hagar aside, we have here a marvellous example of the freshwater springs at oasis throughout the Middle East. Dammit, the oases are fault controlled—what can't you understand about that? Just to shut up the opposition, that thousand-gallon-per-day spring at Jericho is probably on a fault that appears to be one of a parallel series on the west side of the Dead Sea. Know that the Yiddish real estate salesmen don't want you to know that, but before you buy, go to the Geological Survey of Israel and ask, "Where are the faults?"

So, dearest reader, what we are left with is the nature of all of those beautiful photos of palm trees gracing the banks of all those oases. What it actually means is that some primal earth fracture has brought fresh water to the surface, but many of those fractures are faults and faults can move, and if they do, they are earthquakes, so the water comes with a price. Maybe not today, but sometime.

Don't believe me, but stomp into the Geological Survey of Israel and demand to know the fracture pattern in your area of interest. If they give you the run around, threaten to expose them on YouTube.

What I find so extraordinary is that we have known the story of Hagar and the well for perhaps 3,800 years, wherein two of the world's great religions have been founded, yet we have never seemed to connect any of it to how the creator does these things using the implements and resources at hand. We are so self-centred that such things as asteroid impacts and fracturing of the earth is as though it were happening on another planet and has nothing to do with us. Yes, Hagar my dear, it does appear that God's forethought sent an asteroid to crash into central Arabia so that you would not die of thirst, thereby establishing your son as the premier originator of one of the world's great religions. Do you really believe that "God is Great," or is that just some sort of dodge to be in a good position in the interim? My position is that God would never have bequeathed us this big brain if He did not intend for us to use it. My problem arises from the scenario that if we don't use it, will the Almighty just supersede us with someone or something that is not quite so flighty.

This just in from my plethora of research assistants: there was another meteor impact there about six hundred years ago. Holy St. Bartholomew, it seems as if the almighty has this place in the crosshairs. I thought that meteors would never strike the same place twice, but two impacts quite close together (in geological time) must be more than just coincidence. So what next? I won't even venture a guess, but my advice for pilgrims to Mecca might be to take along a telescope and a suitcase seismograph.

Geology can make some very practical explanatory insights possible, but just because we might be able to explain the mechanics of earthly contortions does not project much of a reason for why the tired old earth does what it does, when it does it. Just don't be telling God what he can or cannot do, or with what tools. Time now, though, to get back to the main storyline before we lose it completely.

Part of the explanation for Noah's story lies in the PhD thesis of a geology student at the University of Calgary, Dr. Darcy Gregg.

Ever since the petroleum industry hit the Canadian prairies, geologists have speculated about the fracture patterns obvious on their air photos. In her lecture to the Calgary Mineral Exploration Group, Darcy explained: Apparently one can see the same fracture pattern on the surface of Venus, which has never seen water, and therefore never known erosion, so the fractures are as fresh as the day they were fraqued. Darcy's explanation utilizes the dynamic effects of centrifugal force on a flexible ball with a solid skin to explain how these fractures occur. The ball (earth) compresses at the poles (23 miles) and expands at the equator, so something has to give in that hard, brittle shell. The result is a series of 45-degree fractures, which develop to relieve the stress. Darcy calls these fractures the orthogonals. They propagate through later sediments as the earth grunts and groans around in orbit. She didn't mention the longitudinals (N-S) or the latitudinals (E-W, see photo) in her talk, but I have encountered all three in the field.

Indeed, the Crowsnest Pass deflection in British Columbia is likely a latitudinal, which is responsible for one of the world's great base metal mines, the Sullivan at Kimberly, BC. Darcy claims that the orthagonals are responsible for the localization of many of the reef oil reservoirs in Alberta, not to mention possibly the diamond pipes of the Buffalo Head Hills. Okay, Dr. Gregg, we're paying attention, and just to prove it, we'll draw that diagram.

So now what does all this have to do with Noah's flood? Glad you asked! Despite the ramifications of angry Gods, there still must be a mechanism. That's where geologists become useful—sometimes we will have to involve ourselves in a bit of detail.

We can reasonably place the North Anatolia fault (see map of Anatolia, Turkey) almost along the fortieth parallel of latitude, more or less along the Araxes River in eastern Turkey, and just south of Lake Mangas and Ulubot (Apolyant), offsetting the eastern branch of the Susurlu River as well as the Sakarga River in western Turkey. It probably enters the Aegean Sea just south of the Dardanelles, passes between the islands of Simbroy and Lemas, and becomes lost at sea. Every time the subduction burps, the North Anatolia fault moves—big time.

If we then look at the landscapes of north western Turkey, we notice that many of the river valleys, plus the Dardanelles, mostly bear in a northeast-southwest direction, that is, along Dr. Gregg's orthogonals. Now add a brutal big east-west fault (not a latitudinal, as it is caused by the subduction), and we have a recipe for disaster: subduction moves, North Anatolia fault moves, orthogonal moves—a chain reaction all down the line, to effect everything in the area.

Now if we look at the Sea of Marmara, its shores are pretty well east-west with the two long inlets or arms bearing east. One might reasonably say that these inlets are parallel to the main fault and are related to it and doubtlessly active in the past. They may even be splays of the main fault and thereby subject to movement anytime the main one moves. Ryan and Pitman suggest (P 158 *Noah's Flood*)[23] that one or other of these eastern branches may have been the Black Sea inlet/outlet prior to the last glacial maxima. There is even an indentation in the contour of the Black Sea shelf to support such a claim. Of course, after the very arid times of the glacial maxima that water course would not have been available as an avenue for refilling the Black Sea basin once the level of the Mediterranean and Aegean Seas rose again when the ice melted, because the Sakarga River valley would have been blown full of sand. Just remember this little item (See Chapter 6) for the last final chapter of this book – no, no hints yet).

---

23 Ryan and Pitman, *Noah's Flood* (Toronto: Simon and Schuster, 2000), 158.

Then, the Arabian and/or African plate lurched northward. That activated the Anatolia fault, which opened the long comatose fractures across the Bosphorous Ridge. If we look closely at these fractures, the northern half of the Bosphorous Strait shows two intersecting orthoganals (thanks, Dr. Gregg). Then there is about a quarter of the remaining distance that could be construed as a longitudinal, ending up with a short strip that is probably another orthogonal, which sort of defines the coastline to the southwest along the waterfront of Constantinople (Istanbul). Now, old wounds never really heal, do they? So just wrench that Bosphorous Ridge around a little and you've opened up those fractures that go back to the very beginnings of time on a solid earth (considerably more than six thousand years). The fault is east side up, west side down, so the salt water from the Sea of Marmara and all seas to the south, rushed in, increasing the flow daily as the soft rock yielded to the tumultuous force of the inrushing water. There are some estimates that the waterfall may have been over 400 feet high above the gorge. If you look at the Niagara Gorge in Ontario, it is only about ten miles long, but it eroded over millennia through very hard rock. The Bosphorous is half again longer, but it cut through much softer rock, which had been mutilated over eons by the effects of the North Anatolia fault, so it eroded very quickly. Some references suggest that the amplitude of the sound of the eroding water would have been like that of a roaring bull.

So God's warning to Noah may not have been of the more prosaic voice from the clouds genera but that of a huge earthquake and the bull roaring waterfall. ("Holy Toledo, Noah, if that keeps up, we are going to be flooded out.")

We probably need to pause here for a minute to recognize other geologists who don't completely agree with me and Ryan and Pitman. How could they not? Well, you may come in contact with their take on the story, so I will present their view as befits one of the scientific persuasion, even if they are wrong. Well, maybe not entirely wrong, but perhaps just a little. You know what science people are like, but you are going to have to bear with us for a couple of pages.

When the great glaciers built to their maximum the appalling weight of the ice pushed the crust of the earth further down in to the liquid mantle. According to Newton's third law, to every action, there is an equal and opposite reaction. So, when the ice front began to retreat northward, the depressed land could come back up. Remember isostatic rebound—slow and measured. It took a while, perhaps even millennia. So when one tries to establish age dates for land-based goings on from the isotopes in ice cores (*Why the West Rules - For Now*, Morris p 83),[24] one is using very temperamental atmospheric based measures to predict a rock mantle based response, and there may be a considerable time lag. This digression is aimed at the theory that the Black Sea's trough was filled with fresh water from the humungous melt water lake east of Warsaw, Poland, being dumped into the Dnepr River to flood down in to the Black Sea trough when the ice melted and the land rebounded to empty the lake. I'm not saying this didn't happen—it obviously did—but it was a delayed response. Probably so much so that the shifting of the earth's crust not only dumped the lake but was reflected in activating faults of the entire Middle East subduction zone, so that the Black Sea may actually have been being filled with fresh water from the north and the salt water from the south at about the same time. No wonder the flood was so urgent—both taps were on.

So thanks guys for reminding me, but here's a review of the key: the isostatic rebound will have activated the whole Middle Eastern subduction zone, so prepare for other floods as well. Remember what we said back in the chapter on glaciation: the Younger Dryas (that millennial long cold snap after the glaciers started to melt) was probably due to Lake Agassi over in Manitoba dumping its cold fresh water into the Great Lakes and down the St. Lawrence to disrupt the Gulf Stream. Well, that happened some two millennia after the glaciers melted, so postulating a millennia or two delay for a similar procedure at the Warsaw Lake is not unreasonable. One major difference, though, is that Lake Agassi was nowhere near any subduction zone, so there was no big attendant faulting like we probably had in the Middle East to set up other flooding scenarios (as in the case of the Warsaw Lake, which probably simply spilled into the already filling bucket that was the Black Sea). Glaciation is truly the Handmaiden of God, is it not?

---

24 Ian Morris, *Why the West Rules For Now:* (Toronto: McClelland & Steward, 2011, 83.

And, yes, perhaps all these floodwater goings on might not leave enough time to construct a boat the size of a modern cruiser out of gopher wood with stone tools. It would, however, leave time enough to build quite a fleet of reed boats to accommodate most of the extended family, their seeds, some livestock, and precious artefacts in numerous ARCS (safe boxes). I'm going with the roaring of the waterfall as the odds-on-favourite warning device. Noah was no dummy, as he subsequently proved. Besides, he had that beautiful blond Amorite wife, who, if the later scribes had not been so chauvinistic, would have been given full credit for her role in the drama. And God aside, what a fantastic love story. But we digress! This is supposed to be a geological treatise, not a female appreciation program. What bothers me a little about us raconteurs is that we always seem to have to go over the edge to make things seem more heroic than they actually are, when in anyone's ken, my tale of Noah should be heart stopping and believable. We're a strange lot, we *Homo sapiens*; so often our thought processes are not so ordinal and sequential as we might like to believe. More often than not we fixate on one idea and then, like the proverbial snake oil salesman, reorder, add or delete, and twist everything to suit the perspective that we have decided on in advance. But in so doing, we run roughshod over the truth and items of evidence that could really matter to an intellectually acceptable outcome. As quoted by *The Economist* (Oct. 2010), "When history becomes scripture and men deities, it is the truth that suffers." So I should probably insert here an apologetic reference to an item that has been allowed to fuzzify the interpretation and understanding of Noah's story for far too long. To wit, we biblical scholars are probably guilty of fixating on one interpretation of Noah's flood, that of it having been caused by intense rain (chapter 7, verse 12, KJV): "And the rain was on the earth forty days and forty nights and the windows of heaven were opened." But we conveniently overlook another important verse (7:11): "On that day all of the fountains of the great deep were broken up"

I admit that that line would not make much sense to my non-geologically trained fellows. But to me, it is quite obvious: an earthquake opened the orthogonal fractures in the Bosphorus Ridge (broken up), and the waters of the Mediterranean surged in (fountains of the great deep). So for my money, if you are open to interpreting the wording of the ancients, you can construct a reasonable picture of what happened. And blame us, not the ancients; they had no concept of geological processes, but we do, and it behoves us to acknowledge that we can only be so brilliant, because we are standing on the shoulders of giants.

Perhaps in retrospect, "how odd of God to choose the Jews," or the Moslems, or the Middle East for that matter, as a venue for the greatest agricultural experiment and the civilizations that resulted. But just don't be telling God what to do—you're not that smart. It is, truly though, about the last place on the planet that I would have chosen, but perhaps it was the winner because it was on the Grand Trunk route out of Africa or just because the vicissitudes of challenge makes tough customers of us all. God help today's youth. Whenever I think of what a paltry little *Homo sapiens* I have been, I think of those giants, Noah, Abraham, Moses the King of Surrapak or Gilgamesh (see next chapter), and the honour that I must do them to make this the best job I can possibly do in the area of knowledge that the good Lord may have apportioned me.

The Garden of Eden story sounds just a little bit like a real estate agent I know (bear with us, pilgrim, and all will eventually be made clear). Note: location of Garden of Eden from *Legend* by David Rohl—p55.[25] Lake Van and Lake Urmia, I believe, are just a touch on the salty side, not from the flood but because of leaching sodium chloride out of the rocks around there—sediments of the ancient Tethys Sea. Because salt has played such a very large role in our legends, we should take time to mention that that whole Middle East area was a shallow sea, or evaporate basin, back before Pangea broke up. So there is an awful lot of salt around, whether it be in the Dead Sea 1,300 feet below today's sea level or in Lake Van 6,000 feet above, depending on which side of the subduction fault you are on. We could spend an entire chapter on the fascinating structural geology of the area but would probably lose most of our readers.

---

25 David Rohl, *Legend: The Genesis of Civilization* (Mississauga: Random House, 2000), 55.

Just one short jab at us modern know-it-alls: thousands of years ago a universal flood was a pretty likely explanation for why there was so much salt around, so careful with your superior modern knowledge, Bunko. In addition, at over 6,000 feet, there must be some fairly frosty nights in December, certainly nothing like the balmy climate of the Black Sea shelf. Garden of Eden sounds like a bit of a sales pitch to me, but then, those gallant Hebrews didn't stay up there all that long. Perhaps the condos were leaky, or there was crop failure, or Mama just yearned for the seashore, or "I'm just not going to stay another year in this God-forsaken hole!" In whatever case, the Hebrews migrated south, sort of like permanent snow birds.

We moderns tend to maintain a bit of a hierarchical aversion to walking great distances, except for the purpose of competition, but that was generally the preferred method of travel for the ancients. The Plains Indians in Alberta used to trade with the Woodland Cree along the Black Wolf trail, which was a 250-mile weekend jaunt along what is today Highway No. 2 north (the Queen Elizabeth Highway). Another rather wistful tale was trade westward between the plains Blackfoot and the interior Kootenay tribes. When the forestry were bulldozing a road up the Old Man River, they came on this large mound of gravel, and without putting a lot of thought into it they dozed the whole thing into the grade. Turns out that every time an Indian runner made the trip across the mountains, he would throw a stone on to the pile. That little pile of gravel represented hundreds of thousands of trips over the mountains on foot. So, doubtlessly, our Hill County Hebrews would have known of the wonderful attractions of the big cities to the southeast, "down on the delta," a distance as the crow flies of only 700 miles down the Tigris River Valley or the shorter but more treacherous route through the Zagros Mountains.

When Abraham's predecessors arrived in Ur, they encountered another flood story not dissimilar from their own. Certain elements of the two stories seem to have become interchangeable. Well, a flood, after all, is a flood. There are always a lot of common features—people drown, habitations get swamped, and the guys with the boats survive. It is the telling of the tale, decades, centuries, and millennia later, that "gets the business." So, because we have such a reasonable and somewhat factual set of explanations so readily at hand, we will use them to authenticate the two flood concepts to cheer and mourn our brave forefathers and mothers who had no inkling of faults, fractures, glaciers, or sand dams. Perhaps they were actually fortunate, because other than the prophets predicting dire events, they didn't spend a lot of time worrying about the next geological cataclysm.

I believe that I will have given enough of a geological background in this chapter that subsequent explanations may enjoy enough of a scientific basis so that the reader will not entirely reject them out of hand. It is perhaps not that difficult to integrate the scientific, religious, and legendary if one can only tap into one's pool of good will, in order to hear me out and perhaps take a firm position at a later time. I do not believe that the different approaches are necessarily mutually exclusive. A love affair with Mother Earth does not necessarily negate other perspectives—it's all of a piece.

The geological perspective on the Middle East is not that much less convoluted than the religious and political aspects. The breakup of the supercontinent and subduction of the African and Arabian plates has rendered the place a hotbed of lesser geological processes all the way from the very beginning of time on earth, as represented by the orthogonal fractures, through "the big chill" of glaciation with the tying up of much of the planet's moisture in glacial ice, through the normalization of climate, to the persistent earthquakes. What a spot to choose to civilize that naked ape. Yahweh, what were you thinking?! But just as with our shibboleths of today, "if you want a job done, pick a busy person." Perhaps if you want to speed up evolution, choose a geologically complex venue and just perhaps we don't understand all of it yet. Well, we don't! Who were the little blue men, why Moses in Egypt? What's with the asteroids down by Mecca? Why the two floods? Oooops, almost let the cat out of the bag there. Yes, there may have been passing reference to some of these items before, but I should attempt to cast it all into a grandiose conclusion. Now that we all understand the geological processes applicable, the specifics will be revealed as their turn comes up. But let's do take a little closer look at the epic of Noah before leaving the hills of eastern Turkey and Kurdistan. The Noah story was not totally

Cataclysm

a sea shanty. Yes, they landed on the east coast of the Black Sea, but it got a little convoluted after that.

If you have every listened to your seniors tell their stories, you will recognize that within several generations, the stories transformed gradually toward the heroic. Of course, we wish to believe in the heroics of our predecessors, and no matter what your flat historic perception, their moves were historic for the times, no matter which end of the law they may have been on. The bootleggers of Scotland became the Glenn-whatevers of modern commerce at prohibitive prices to the simple bairns. But what about this chapter that purported to reveal the geological underpinnings of the whole story and ends up back with the Amorite love story? Does that say something about what human intelligence is worth? My background might suggest insights that could make me rich, but I would give it all for one loving kiss from my darling, and she was not even blond.

So don't give me the gears about human intelligence and insight. We know a lot of stuff, but our emotions severely interact and intercept the logic that we might otherwise obtain. If I were Noah, I'd go with my beautiful wife and fight whatever battles came up along the way. "If we don't like the venue, we can always move, sweetheart." It was sort of out of the frying pan into the fire: From Lake Van to Ur along the subduction zone thence over to the Dead Sea fault In the Promised Land, but I see Yahweh's reasoning: toughen them up!

Oh! You want a recap of those geological processes, but just a short one? Okay. First check out the diagram of subduction and then look at the tectonic map. Then note that the African plate is subducting under the European plate, and that is essentially why Greece and Turkey are so mountainous. Also note that when that subduction fault leaves Cypress, it is heading directly for the Big Bend in the Euphrates River and ultimately into the general Lake Van area. Then remember that when the glacial maximum obtained, northern Europe would have been pushed down into the fluid mantle, making it very difficult for the African plate to push under it. But when the ice melted, the crust rebounded, probably making it easier for the African plate to move north so we would have an active phase of faulting and mountain-building, which "shook" open Darcy Gregg's orthogonals and let the Mediterranean waters flood into the Black Sea through the Bosphorus Straits. At or about the same time, isostatic rebound raised the northern plains, dumping the great Warsaw melt water lake down the Dnephr River into the Black Sea. So Noah did not have a lot of time to ponder. His decision was flood-boat, and he and his whole entourage were blown across the Black Sea by the west wind. Others trekked north and west up the river valleys, while still others moved south and east into Anatolia (Turkey) and the Levant (Lebanon).

At about the same time, or even earlier, a somewhat similar scenario was being played out in the Persian Gulf and for much the same reasons, only here the subduction zone lay parallel to the Tigris River and the Persian Gulf. That's all you get of that for now. You have to read the last chapter for the detail—and what detail it is! Hope this short refresher is some help. Geology is a very convoluted study that often requires more faith than proof. The next time you drive from Jasper down Highway 93 (the Icefields Highway) to Calgary, hire me as your guide (at an exorbitant rate), and we will reminisce about Anatolia and what mountain-building can do to and for this naked ape.

But just before we leave this section on geological stuff, I should come clean and put forward another idea that is difficult to prove but intuitively possible. It is perhaps best described by Graham Hancock in *Finger Prints of the Gods*. He locates "the First Time," as in Antarctica, which also serves to locate the Lost Continent. In this theory (speculation), the whole solid crust of the earth fits like the skin of an orange around the more fluid interior layers of the planet. There are a variety of forces acting on this skin—the centrifugal force of a spinning body; the coriolis force, which sort of curves from pole to equator; and the gyroscopic force, which is perpendicular and at 90 degrees to the axis of spin. These are relatively constant. But then there is a pendicular (pendulum) force exerted by the abnormal and off-centre weight of glacial ice in the northern and southern regions. When this latter force becomes sufficiently large and or unbalanced it could cause the entire "skin" of the earth to slip on its fluid underpinnings and thereby relocate all land masses to new and different latitudes and longitudes.

That the ice was off centre and the earth would be unbalanced is really not in question. The ice got as far south as Indianapolis in the eastern United States, but only just into Montana further west. Siberia appears to have been ice free until perhaps the final advance, whereas it came down into the Southern Ukraine (50 degrees) and some say two miles thick over there then. So certainly some great cosmic forces were at work. We don't know as of yet exactly what, or how much, but some day all will be revealed. Perhaps the greatest thing against Hancock's theory is time. Geological processes take time, often large amounts of time. The drift of the North and South American continents westward has taken over 200 million years. So if the earth's skin were to slip it probably would not have happened overnight and overnight is the approximate amount of time, in geological terms, that mankind has been around.

The idea did not originate with Hancock, and indeed the concept has been used to explain the reversal of the magnetic poles every so often. There is not much concrete physical evidence that such a concept is valid, but pretty much anything that can happen will happen. Hancock uses this possibility to account for a lost civilization in the "First Time", which is just a concept of his. I'm not quite so daring, as I don't think that it is necessary to go that far. To my mind there is plenty of space on the exposed shelves of the Mediterranean, Black Sea, and Persian Gulf shelves to accommodate our "First Time" lost, advanced civilization which I just interpret as before the big melt. In fact, there is even some evidence for it: we will note the "capitol" in the fishermen's nets off of the island of Smothrace. (A capitol is the decorative top piece of a column that holds up a roof.)[26] We just haven't done our submarine homework. Not to denigrate Handcock's theory; many geologists give guarded support to the basic idea of a mobile Lithosphere, but won't go the whole distance for lack of concrete evidence, and in my case there is no need to fall back on such way out theorizing. (I should talk!) However, there is the possibility of an advanced civilization in far off Antarctica. We know that 60,000 to 70,000 years ago a gang of Africans walked over to Australia and even navigated perhaps 60

26 Graham Hancock, *Fingerprints of the Gods: The Evidence of Earth's Last Civilizations* (New York: Three Rivers Press, 1995).

miles of water. We also know that as early as 200,000 years ago there was a group of *Homo sapiens* living on the south coast of Africa, so when it came time to move they might have gone south and west to intercept a continent that was then much farther north. It would explain the Piri Reis maps, although they would have shown more detail to the south and less to the north instead of the other way around, with Giza dead centre. Also they can be explained by the sailors described in the final chapter hitting the high seas after "the flood" as well. Recall that Piri Reiss was a Turkish naval officer who discovered these very ancient world maps that showed the east coast of South America as well as Antarctica from before any known Europeans had ever been there. Some say that they would have showed more detail to the south and less to the north if they had been made by southerners; also, they are centred on Giza in Egypt. No one has any idea how often they may have been grafted on to some pre-existing cartographer's work, but since they are centred on Giza it is reasonable to assume that that is their origin.

Actually Gavin Menzie's book *The Lost Empire of Atlantis* is considerably more realistic. [27] His explanation of the volcanoes on Santorini being responsible for dispatching the Minoen society fits the geological picture of subduction of the African plate much better than any other way out speculation.

So no, I think that the jury is really out on that one, but it is something to keep in mind as the ice melts and we can see what is on the dry land of the Antarctic continent.

We would very much like to fall back on the National Geographic's gene study to prove the in and out migrations of the Northwest Black Sea shelf, but the period of settlement was so short that it is unlikely to have had much permanent impact on the genome. We are more into the realm of anthropologists and archaeologists, and that's a slow, painful, and expensive route. But there is some pretty good speculation already with regard to where various groups come from and how they got there. Most walked, but Noah the navigator was a bit before his time (perhaps!) and somewhat of a precursor of things to come.

27 Menzies, *Lost Empire of Atlantis*.

Integrating the geological processes with all the 'human' stuff that was going on does not 'perhaps' paint a simple somewhat more complex picture. The geology is pretty straight forward (to a geologist). The huge glaciers pushed the surface of the earth down. When they melted, it sprang back up, causing faulting and earthquakes which flooded the Black Sea. What happened to the inhabitants is a matter of conjecture. We do have some hints in our legends, scriptures and archaeology; some fled up to the river valleys, some probably walked overland into Turkey and the Levant. The most engaging reference is that of Noah and his "Arc" and their flight across the Black Sea.

QUESTIONS FOR GEOLOGY CHAPTER

1. Continental drift and subduction sounds like a fairy story. How can you prove it?
2. If the level of the Black Sea has risen so much, is there any chance of ever locating the old speculated settlements on the shelf, and what stage of development might they have been in?
3. Why was there such a thing as the Tethys Sea?
4. The pilgrimage over the Camino in Northern Spain is 800 km. Why is there not, at least, a Jewish pilgrimage from Lake Van down the Tigris River to Abadan?
5. Is there any geological study of the meteor impact in central Arabia?
6. How accepted is Dr. Gregg's thesis of orthogonal fractures?
7. Are there any learned studies about the subduction zones in the Middle East, or are you just shooting from the hip?
8. What other studies are there that might lend support to the present thesis?

CHAPTER 5:   NOAH, ET AL.

RIGHT OFF THE TOP we're going to assume that the reader has at least a nodding acquaintance with the biblical story of Noah's Ark. For those not brought up in the Christian tradition, that may be a bit of a leap, but in a nutshell, God spoke to Noah and told him that because mankind had been so sinful, He was going to drown 'em all by making it rain for forty days and forty nights to flood the earth. But because Noah was a good man he would be elected to survive, provided that he built a great boat (ark) and herded onboard a male and female of every species of animal on earth, which he did. Then after the deluge the Ark landed on Mt. Ararat in what is now Eastern Turkey.

The story of Noah and his Arc is perhaps the most beloved of all biblical stories. It's beautifully illustrated in my old child's Bible. What the tale lacks in accuracy is more than made up for in beautiful narrative and the illustrator's imagination. But in our age of disbelievers and a "show me the meat" approach to everything, we can still salvage a bit of a true epic tale of bravery in the face of bewildering astronomical cataclysm that would dazzle the most proficient architect of fiction. But this is not fiction—it actually happened. Perhaps not quite the way the scribes embellished it, but there was a big-time cataclysm. What a colossal historical item! Those unbelievers need only kick back, and I will indeed show them the meat. But why bother? Well, I do have to admit to an ulterior motive. I persuaded most—or at least some, I hope—that they needed a minimal acquaintance with glaciation in order to get a feel for from whence we came. Well, now I'm pulling the same con job on understanding the concept of massive flooding that is present in the folklore of peoples around the world who lived near the seacoasts when the glaciers melted.

It may be a timely item to point out two concepts of good and evil that existed in the ancient world. In the Hebrew version, good appears to have been a broad judgment as to what would be "good" for all "men." In most other groups at the time, good was more of a relative thing. Good meant that if you thought differently, it would be fairly easy to extrapolate that concept to suit the position in which the scribes, who were recording events for posterity, may have found themselves. They would have to appear consistent with the accepted conventional wisdom and the good of their masters, who in most cases would not have been of the Hebrew persuasion. Sort of the old Scottish idea of "he who pays the piper calls the tune."

We should probably begin with a rough dating of the Noah episode. As alluded to later, Noah's fifteen minutes of fame probably happened some 7,500 years ago.[28] It is important to note that this was still in the Neolithic (new Stone Age) era. The Bronze Age wasn't due for perhaps another 1,000 to 2,000 years, but consciousness had been visited on *Homo sapiens* some 70,000 years previously. So, Noah was no hunter-gatherer—well, maybe a little. As we proposed in the previous chapter, the exposed shelves around the Mediterranean and Black Seas were very fertile, and prior to the ice melting they may have encouraged the halting beginnings of agriculture. This may have been particularly true around the west and north west shores of the Black Sea, where the estuaries of the Danube, Sirel, Prutul, Dnestr, Bug, Dnepr, and Don Rivers make for a veritable haven for plant, animal, and aquatic life, and the estuaries flowed out across the emergent shelf some 80 to 100 miles wide. If I were going to plant any Garden of Eden that would certainly be the pick of possible venues in the near east. It is all under water now, but not back in Noah's day. Archaeologists tend to like to "dig and sift"—submarine archaeology is still in its infancy—but it is my bet that the northwest shelf of the Black Sea will prove to be a prehistoric treasure trove. Estuaries seem to have been prime real estate to settle down and

---

28 Ryan and Pitman, *Noah's Flood*.

raise a family. There was probably good fishing, certainly fertile soil, and the herbivores definitely wouldn't need an invitation. In the case of this particular venue, it seems to have been at least the interim destination of those beautiful blond giants—the Amorites (chapter 6, verse 4, King James Version: "there were giants on the earth in those days"). Just a word of caution here, though: ancient peoples tended to be quite small, so giants to them might not seem extraordinary to us, probably six feet or more tall—think Scandinavians or Wotouis. But why were they called Amorites? Well, the Roman God of love was Amor, and when we are feeling rather more than "in like," we are said to be amorous, so one might assume these big blondies must he been pretty good looking too. At least Noah thought so, as he is believed to have taken one for his wife. So this is not to be just the tale of an historic trek but a love story as well. (Actually Amorite just means "Westerner.")

So where did the Neolithic settlers of the Black Sea shelf come from? The National Geographic says that most of us Europeans carry a gene from central Asia, but as nearly as I can make out, that may have come in somewhat later. National Geographic does admit to part of the Diaspora from Africa having perhaps traveled along the south shore of the Mediterranean. Okay, I can accept that, but in my version when they come to the straits of Gibraltar, they crossed the five-mile interval and settled in on the exposed shelves of Spain and France, and when the rising Mediterranean flooded them out, they fled up the Rhone River valley, then up the Doubs River to Freiburg, and then over the hump to the Danube and down to the Black Sea. Or across northern Italy to the Sava River, then to the Danube, and then to the Black Sea. In fact, this is just the reverse of what most archaeologists believe, namely, that the migration was from east to west. In either case, it took many centuries, even millennia, providing lots of time to whiten out. And remember, the Black Sea didn't flood for perhaps five thousand years after the big melt.

So who is to cast the first stone at Noah for taking one of these beautiful Amorites to wife? The Hebrews probably became a white race, taller than the average at the time, just because of his preference for blonds. Well, now that we've settled the genetics, let's get on with the daring do. We shan't get into a lot of the boring daily life on the Black Sea shelf. We just wish to establish that through whatever mechanism, Noah knew of an impending flood and took appropriate action—he built a boat. But how did he know? Yeah, yeah, God told him, but how?

My wife was a very inspired elementary school teacher, and she used to maintain that every once in a while she would get a kid who just "knew stuff" from no traceable background. She called them "redheaded strangers" (from the western song "Rode into Town One Night"). Nostradamus was doubtless one of these, as probably were many of the Biblical prophets. So do you suppose that there may have been a redhead amongst the blond Amorites and God spoke through him? A more likely scenario is presented in the section on geology. Doesn't really matter—we're onto the shipyard now—but we are going to have to indulge in some revisionism there. This is the Neolithic Era. Metal isn't due for another one or two thousand years, so without metal tools to split the gopher wood into planks and some sort of metal fasteners to hold them together, the ark, as portrayed didn't exist. I mean, the dimensions given are the size of a modern cruiser. This is only the first time we will have occasion to note evidence for the oral tradition being considerably embellished when written down, probably four or five thousand years later, by scribes in Ur of the Chaldeans, who knew nothing of the Black Sea or its Neolithic sailors. But that makes the story even more enticing. These were Neolithic heroes of the highest caliber, but their craft will have been a boat built from reeds and held together by other reeds in that intricate professionalism of the boat builders of prehistory. The scribes who did the transcribing sound as though they probably weren't even Hebrew, because ark in Hebrew means "safe place." Remember the Ark of the Covenant? It was a box. So, how big was the reed boat? Well, those used by the Neolithic sailors in the Red Sea, the "battleships," would hold perhaps a couple of handfuls of people cheek to jowl. And no, Noah wasn't 600 years old. I'm scarcely one ninth that tenure, and I can hardly nail a board on the back fence! So, once we get by the Cecil B. DeMille version of the voyage, we have such a heroic human undertaking as to be positively breathtaking. They set sail with all of their precious things in a box, probably including einkorn seed, obsidian knives, and the missus shell beads (einkorn was wild wheat not corn, as we know it, which came later from Central America). There were the kids, of course, a goat or two, some doves (okay, we can eat them if times get tough), no chickens yet—they were jungle fowl from the east—and a goatskin of beer to see Noah through the rough weather. Although there were no pigs chapter 7, verse 2, says that they did take some "unclean" animals—just why is unclear, because there were no elephants or giraffes, let alone platypus, koala bears, or kangaroos. Now those reed boats were not diesel powered, so some wag or other has calculated that the voyage may well have taken forty days and forty nights. As I make it, it was a 650-mile trip. Now, in any man's language, that is a pretty courageous thing to do in a raft made of straw, even if your beautiful blond wife agrees to come along. So presumably they must have been very much in love; perhaps she was even pregnant. So these two lovers would have been hero and heroine in any epoch, and therefore there is no need to guild the lily. There are all sorts of tales from around the world about this flood. The articulate settlers of the Middle East have simply drawn the flooding to our attention with superior storytelling acumen. The good king down south just had to survive the tidal wave and walk inland, so why did Noah choose this treacherous route? Seems as if he may have been under some pressure from hostiles, likely his wife's relatives—the Amorites. They were big, strong, and perhaps not entirely accepting of the little Jewish guy. ("Well, I told her not to marry him!") Anyway, apparently Noah thought it the better part of valour to move on—big time—and his darling wife came with him, against all odds (see Prairie Voles in previous chapter on glaciation). How many of our wives would come along if their harebrained "God-loving" husbands were about to embark on an epic journey like that with all her relatives badmouthing her decision of the heart? I think Mrs. Noah has been given very short shrift in all this. Give me that girl any day over those other stay-at-home Amorite hussies.

But what did happen to the Amorites? They sort of disappeared from history, unless our previous speculation of a grand trek north is correct. It sort of tickles my fancy that my son-in-law was the product of a Finnish mother and a Jewish father, who had to run from the tidal wave of Fascism as it swept over Europe in the 1940s.

I don't know whether you call that six degrees of separation or what goes around comes around.

Actually, though, a lot of the Amorites appear again, within the Syrian empire or Babylonia. But poor old Noah didn't have the advantage of modern science to tell him what was happening, and apparently God, however he communicated, was pretty short on detail. So we have had to wait for another 7,500 years for a couple of oceanographers from Woods Hole to tell us actually what may have happened. Well, okay, I'll fill in a little of the geological stuff.

In their 1998 book *Noah's Flood,* Ryan and Pitman (any Newfoundlanders in the audience?) imply that Noah et al. were probably living on the shelf at the west end of the Black Sea, west or southwest of the Crimean peninsula. The level of both the Mediterranean and Black Seas had dropped significantly, the Mediterranean because the general ocean level had dropped (it was still connected through the Straits of Gibraltar, though) and the Black Sea because it was cut off from the Mediterranean. The glaciers had sucked much of the water out of the atmosphere, so there was little rainfall to fill the rivers to fill the Black Sea, so it would have become a Great Salt Lake. Perhaps not even so great. I don't think that we have any measure of how much the level may have fallen, but certainly lots of fertile shelf was exposed for thousands of years and hundreds of miles.

Okay, now it gets a little complicated, but bear with us. As previously mentioned, the original connection between the Black Sea and the Mediterranean at the Sea of Mamara may not have been the same one that we see today—the Bosporus Strait. It perhaps doesn't matter much, except that it could underscore another event perhaps somewhat familiar, even distantly related, nearly 2,000 miles to the southeast. No, not going to tell you yet!

The Bosporus Strait is, of course, the present-day connection between the Black Sea and the Sea of Mamara, which is then connected to the Mediterranean through the Dardanelles. Remember that? Perhaps a little review is in order. The Sea of Mamara has two eastern branches, both of which may be related to the Anatolia fault. The most southerly of these branches looks to have been the locus of the ancient Sakargo River, which today dumps into the

Black Sea. The most northerly branch of the Sea of Mamara was probably the original connector between the Sea of Mamara and the Black Sea. The Bosporos Strait, which sort of perpendicularly bisects the east-west ridge, probably wasn't even there or at least just a break in the ridge before the flood. So when the Mediterranean rose again twelve thousand years ago, there was no channel to the Black Sea, because—remember what we said about high winds—over the twenty thousand years of the glacial maxima, dust storms had plugged off the old channel with sand. Remember this!

In the 1990s we were given a firsthand demonstration of what a brute the Anatolia fault of NW Turkey is. When these huge intercontinental plate faults move there is hell to pay. Most often, they relax rein on other fractures in the earth's crust, which are then free to open up. Without again getting into a big diatribe about original fracture patterns of a consolidating young earth, the Bosporus would appear to belong to a set of those ancient earth fractures. So the Bosporus "fracture" could have been a feature just waiting for the opportunity to express itself. The Uskudar or east side of the Bosporus fault appears to be the up side and the west or Istanbul side the down side, but it is an entirely new route. The original outlet of the Black Sea, the Sakorga River, was "pirated" by the Bosphorus fracture. The Dardanelle Straits to the southwest appear to belong to a similar set of fractures. They conceivably could have opened at the same time as the Bosporus but were probably there before. Logic would have us believe that they had been there for a long time, as the drainage route for the Marmara Sea. So what I (and Ryan and Pitman) are proposing is that the Black Sea did not refill immediately on melting of the ice up north, because the old channel was filled with sand and the new one had not yet opened, even though the Mediterranean had risen to its pre-glacial level, as its connection to the Atlantic, through the Straits of Gibraltar, remained open. What I am proposing is not quite what Ryan and Pitman said. According to them, some ancient text that they came across described the event as the cascading of the waters from the Mediterranean as "like unto the roaring of a bull" through what I am calling the newly opened Bosporus fracture. And of course, they place the time at around 7,500 years ago.

Some spoilsport geologist from the University of Toronto and other venues too numerous to mention debate this interpretation, because they say that some of the sediments indicate that the flow was in the opposite direction. I caution about their interpretation, because of a forgotten reference to "overfilling" of the Black Sea when the rains came back and the rivers once again disgorged their aqueous load into the Black Sea Basin (remember isostatic rebound). That excess outflow would have reached a balance in subsequent years when the water cycle settled down, and again Ryan and Pitman describe the flow through the Bosporus to be south on the surface and north at depth. It is still, however, an item of controversy and everyone has the right to be wrong.

I am prone to the fault movement scenario, as I will use it in the next chapter to devastating effect. It does seem like this may have been one of those times when the earth suffers the nervous Nellies, not unlike today, when there are big multiple events. I'm going with Robert Ballard, who found ancient shorelines 300 feet down off of Turkey and dated shells and tool worked timbers at 7,500 years ago.

But let's not get too full of our great insightful technical skill and knowledge. Both Noah and the King of Suruppak (next chapter) were warned by their separate gods of impending disaster. So how did that happen? Did they have geologists on the payroll? Probably not! However, there have always been these super smart people around (redheaded strangers) who seem to have an in with the gods. They just seem to know stuff that none of us ordinaries even notice, like, "Good gracious, if that sand dam or fault ever gives way, we are in a passel of trouble." Yes! Concede to the Hebrew view of prophets (with red hair—that's how you can tell 'em). Anyway, both Noah and the King of Suruppak were warned in time. Now, best that we get back to the main storyline.

We sit here and marvel at such an intelligent universe, but if you are the local purveyor of the oral tradition, that's not going to be good enough to hold your audience in awe. If you try to tell them that Noah built a straw raft, put his precious things in a box, packed up the wife and kids, and headed fast out across the Great Salt Lake, most of them will be off to McDonald's for a burger and fries. But back in that chauvinistic era, the omniscience of the deity would have had a lot more traction than a love story. After all, the deity could smite you if you didn't wise up. But I challenge any of today's males to say that they wouldn't be in love with Noah's wife, the consummate supportive female—and blond to boot.

Now, God's flood warning seems to have been pretty urgent, so there probably wasn't much time to come and go—two shifts on the reed boat construction, and that damn fault is just sitting there waiting, perhaps already sprung and under the devil's control. It is the warning of the coming cataclysm that is so poignant. Both gods, the Hebrew Yahweh and the Mesopotamian Ea, were Johnny on the spot, giving appropriate warning for the two men (Noah and the King of Surrapak) to build themselves escape vehicles. Sort of has a modern ring, doesn't it? Then later on in our journey, these two very separate antecedents come together in the City of Ur of the Chaldesse and the two separate stories get mixed up.

Seems like I am always finding fault with the detail of the King James Version of the Bible, but that is truly not the objective. With a little messaging and application of some modern principles, we can render the central core of the text believable to all-comers. Such is the story of Adam and Eve and the Garden to Eden. You might justifiably question why we are jumping from Noah to the story of Adam and Eve. Well, there are some disconnects there that require addressing. The first is the location of the Garden of Eden, very well described in Genesis 2, verses 10–14[29], KJV, as being around Lake Van. The proto-Hebrews never got there until after the flood some 7,500 years ago.[30] So, no, what Adam and Eve are remembering was a much earlier time, when their forefathers and foremothers were hunter-gatherers—dear only knows where. Noah was already a farmer when he and his tribe arrived at the east end of the Black Sea (chapter 9, verse 20). Why the chroniclers had to get him drunk on his own wine to expedite the story is anybody's guess—let's just chalk it up to poetic license. But the story of Adam and Eve are two different stories melded together by some clever craftsmen. The first is the tale of the hunter-gatherers and what an idealistic

---

29 *Holy Bible, The; King James Version*: (Nashville: Thomas Nelson, 1982).
30 Rohl, *Legend*, 53.

life style they lived. Even today, anthropologists maintain that the hunter-gatherers probably only hunted and gathered about three to four hours a day, with no union dues. No one has ventured what they may have done with the rest of their time, but the population did increase quite dramatically. Adam and Eve appear to pine for the "good old days." There is not much reflection on when the game went elsewhere, and the raspberry crop failed. Although that may sound a little viscous, it is a light treatment of some of the horrifying situations that hunter-gatherers faced.

There is such a poignant artefact up on the coast of Baffin Island not far from Pond Inlet. There is a fairly narrow passage between the Borden Peninsula on the NE coast of Baffin Island and Bilot Island just to the east. It has long been a favourite hunting ground for the Inuit (Thule), because the shifting ice in the strait opens Polanya (cracks) in the ice where seals come out to do whatever seals do. The hunting is stupendous, and the only competition is the polar bears, and they are too busy gorging themselves to be a real danger. The Inuit build winter shelters of whalebone and sealskin on shore and everyone gets fat. Except that every once in a while, the Polanya don't open, meaning no seals and everyone starves to death. There are three levels of whalebone and sealskin shelters there, built one on top of the other. So Eve's pining for the good old days may have overlooked, in hindsight, when things didn't go so well. Perhaps this was a case of wilful nostalgia, neglecting to remember when things weren't so great. It was great until it wasn't, and then you were dead. That was what the agricultural revolution was all about—maybe you had to work harder, but at least you were alive. Recall another item, the tree of knowledge (chapter 2, verse 17, KJV). We have pretty good evidence for the coming of consciousness 50,000 to 100,000 years ago, so that is a long time ago for Eve to be musing about. What is so amazing is that their awareness of this epochal change in consciousness in humans should have persisted in memory (or oral tradition) for such a very long time. Ask any farmer about the "mark of Cain." As a very urban person said to me after moving out to an idyllic rural venue, to revel in God's freedom, all they ever do out here is work from dawn to dark, and all weekend. Well, Eve dear, perhaps you are onto something, but then we'd probably have to do something about the virility of the wildlife in order to provide for the 6 billion of us that agriculture has encouraged to despoil the planet's surface, not to mention the skunks in the raspberry patch. Sounds like farming and herding to me, Eve. Just don't forget that the coming of consciousness (the tree of knowledge) was viewed as a curse, not a benefit.

Actually, we probably really do need to stop for a minute to address the apparent time problem between Noah and the Garden of Eden story. Detractors have pointed to the apparent disparity in time to detract from either or both narratives. But actually that whole puzzling quirk need not cause any great problem. Eve's soliloquy is just that—a soliloquy. She bemoans their present hard work requirements compared to how things used to be back in the good ol' hunter-gatherer days. Perhaps one might accuse Mother Eve of wearing her rose coloured glasses, but nothing more exceptional than that. In addition, there does appear to be a venue problem. We know from the biblical description that the Garden of Eden was up around Lake Van, which places it after Noah's flood, but in her soliloquy, Mother Eve appears to be saying that the real Garden of Eden was back in our hunter-gatherer days, before the curse of the coming of consciousness, or as she more artfully puts it, the "Tree of Knowledge." So basically the only problem is rather good storytelling blending the two venues into one tale. I certainly have no problem with that. The problem I do have is how our darling Eve can recall something that happened 70,000 years before. I suppose it was so momentous that it would be pretty difficult to forget. As well, we must remember that going back to before consciousness was bestowed on *Homo sapiens,* we are reaching back in time to Mitochondrial Eve. Therefore, the mesmerizing conclusion I'm coming to is that there appears to be more than memory involved here. I originally sort of jokingly suggested two Eves—but did they know each other? Well, no, but the later mother Eve does seem to have known *about* the former. Bless me! Now there's one for the archaeologists to explain. Okay, so no one is going to believe much of anything about this little rant, so you explain it.

This view of the biblical Eve then allows Noah's Flood to have been contained within the Black Sea, and all's right with the world and our darling legends. Just to remind our readers, those old legends are no more out of line than our modern propensity to make a story as wild as we think we can get away with. I'm on Eve's side. "Ya done good, my darlin."

Another persistent question is why the snake in the Adam and Eve story? Snakes were revered by the ancients as having discovered the secret of eternal life. They thought that shedding of the skin was rebirth and that a snake could go on renewing themselves forever. Now, suddenly, the snake is being reviled. How come? Was it too clever by half, or did the snake meet with someone somewhere on a back road in Louisiana (go look that one up), or is there something even more sinister about this little reversal of fortune? There are no antecedents for this. We are simply hit with it and left to our own devices. But obviously between the time of Euruk and Ur of the Chaldese, something must have happened to denigrate the reptile reputation, or not. Probably the best explanation is the very simple one—that the Tree of Life had always been portrayed with a snake in it by the ancients, probably because of the snake's connection with immorality, and the Hebrew's chronicles simply gave the snake a role to play in the new episode.

One of the items that the scribes of Ur got all screwed up was the landfall of the Ark. And this is quite understandable—those guys were sons of the flatlands, and they were dealing with tales of the mountain tribes. You get a lot of the same disconnect today between the denizens of flatbush in New York and the mountain men of Colorado—or, in my Canadian case, the Gentle Maritimes and the Awesome Rockies. We don't speak the same language. So be gentle in your judgement, dear reader. The sophisticates of Ur had never set foot on the rocky slopes of a mountain, so they knew not of what they were scribing.

No, the Ark (read reed boat) did not come to rest on the slopes of Mt. Ararat. That little hill is 16,941 feet high, an extinct volcano, and 200 miles inland to boot. Even Lake Van is 6,649 feet above sea level, and if you do the geography or read David Rohl's book *Legend,*[31] you will see quite plainly where Genesis 2:10–14 refers to the Lake Van

---

31 David Rohl, *Legend: The Genesis of Civilization:* (Mississauga: Random House, 2000).

area. The logic of the ancients is evident in their supposition that the Ark landed on Mt. Ararat because this is the high point overlooking the salt basin of the very ancient Tethy's Sea. Both Lake Van and Lake Uremia are salty, so the ancient Hebrews assumed that they were vestigial remnants of the flood. But that is not how these lakes got their salt. There just is not enough water on the planet to raise sea level up there. This whole area has been raised from the bottom of an evaporate sea by the action of the subduction of the Arabian plate under the Eurasian plate, thereby raising it up thousands of feet. The salt is leaching out of the sediments that were laid down in that shallow sea that existed prior to the breakup of Pangaea 200 to 250 million years ago. The same thing is true for the Dead Sea in Palestine and the salt domes of Iran. The flood had nothing to do with it, which doesn't mean there wasn't a flood—there was—but not up there. There is another little anomaly that probably should be pointed out at this juncture: Eden is the local name used for the south end of the Persian Gulf, and the word actually means *uncultivated plane*, so the influence of our intrepid wanderers has spread far beyond their original venue.

There are a number of rather obvious disconnects that suggest that our chroniclers did not have degrees in engineering or geography. They present us with the awesome spectacle of the Ark being raised over 6,000 feet, but they then tell us (Genesis 7:20) that the waters rise was 15 cubits, which is about 25 feet. So yes, it does look suspiciously like much of the detail of the story was patched together at a much later time, even perhaps from several different sources, by scriptwriters who had never been there and were getting paid by the "event." The 25 feet appears to have been borrowed directly from the flood on the Persian Gulf, and these writers were within spitting distance of that event, but 1,400 miles as the crow flies, and a passel of mountain ranges from the Black Sea event. But hold on Charlie, just because there are a few quirks in the details doesn't mean the whole tale was invented—it wasn't. Don't go throwing the baby out with the bathwater. I think that we can reasonably establish the flood in the Black Sea, and we have enough outside corroborative evidence of Noah and his blond wife, not to mention we know the geography and ethnography of the eastern end of the Black Sea, that we can eschew the excesses of the scriptwriters and accept the core truth of a mind-boggling epic journey. Wouldn't you males out there just wish that you could fold Noah's beautiful wife onto your chest and reassure her that you would protect her, and how about you ladies? How would you love to have such a hero as Noah to be your mate? No wonder that beauty chose him over her mundane tribal nowhere guys. All we have to do to make sense of history is look at today. Perhaps that is why Cecil B. was so good at making biblical movies—perhaps he belonged to a secret society that had been doing this for millennia!

What we can reasonably say is that Noah took his precious possessions, his beautiful wife, some livestock, and seeds for planting and set out to cross the Black Sea. It probably took about a month. They landed on the eastern shore and took however long to trudge up into the highlands of Lake Van. In the vernacular of the times, that may have been hundreds of years. Once they arrived in the Lake Van area, they may truly be forgiven for believing that they had finally arrived at the Garden of Eden. They settled in and apparently prospered somewhat, but apparently not all that much, because years later they drifted down the Zagros Mountain chain or the Tigris River to the lowlands, where they encountered that incredible urban sophistication of Ur of the Chaldese and left behind forever their simple rural mountain existence. According to the Bible—and who is not going to believe that?—two of Noah's sons, Shem and Ham, had gone down to Ur on a scouting mission prior to the whole tribe descending on this ultra civilized constituency. Apparently Ham stayed with "the old folks" when they finally arrived in or around Ur, but Shem followed "the pirates" over to Upper Egypt (see tale of the pirates in following chapter). Shem's adventure will be what the Hebrew historian Josephus reports as a sort of second Garden of Eden venue for the Hebrews—the fabled Land of Kush in Africa. Whatever happened to that group appears to be lost in the sands of the Nile, as we never hear of them again, as far as I know. Probably just absorption of immigrants. But the most intriguing of the young adventurers was the third son, Jopheth, who apparently went *north*. Now we might conclude that he was his mother's son tall, blond and good looking. We never hear of him again either. But could this be our coveted reference for the origin of the Finns. Some biblical historians claim that all of these names of people, even Noah, simply represent tribal groups.

Well, we know all about the wanderlust of *Homo erectus*, do we not? It really should not be such a stretch of the imagination to understand how the scribes of Ur got the beautiful coming-of-consciousness tale out of the Paleolithic all mixed up with the proto-agricultural event at Lake Van in the Neolithic, but separated by perhaps sixty thousand years. The dramatic inference is how did the coming of consciousness insight exist for 50,000 to 75,000 years to become included in the biblical story. I don't think that we moderns give anywhere near enough credit to the concept of collective understandings or group intelligence (what psychologists might call the collective unconscious) in my perception the power of oral tradition. It did not necessarily have to live in our subconscious, but it was alive in the ancient story telling around the campfire. Did I ever tell you about my recurrent dream of a group of Neoliths dressed in animal skins around a campfire in the Black Forest? Probably, but then you needed reminding, didn't you? Yeah, I know, psychologists will say it's collective unconscious—whatever!

The whole tale is such a beautiful artefact of our "previous life," even when stripped of all of its religious overtones. Just coming out of the recent hunter-gatherer format and moving down to that very sophisticated agrarian civilization of Ur. Well, how are you going to keep them down on the farm once they've been to Paree? These proto-Hebrews would not have been the only ones, but because of their uni-theistic beliefs, they were sufficiently cohesive to hold it all together. What is intriguing is how the biblical stories of this proto-Hebrew tribe lends credence to so much of the other conclusions we have come to from other sources, namely geology and the Gilgamesh.

When Noah and his beautiful wife established somewhere around Lake Van in eastern Turkey, after the flood, they were proto-agriculturists and at least grew grapes on which Noah got smashed (so to speak). But it is the implications provided by the lives of his three sons that is so intriguing for our present story. So we should do a quick review.

Japeth, a tall, blond Amorite, probably took after his mother's side of the family, and so in his journey north his ultimate destination may have been Finland. Shem and Ham appear to have trekked down the Tigris River to Ur of the Chaldees. Shem appears to have stayed there and was probably instrumental in the move of the whole tribe down to lower Mesopotamia some time later. Ham, on the other hand, was a bit more adventurous and took a boat down the Persian Gulf and then over to Africa along much the same route as the "other" flood survivors may have taken decades before (see Chapter 6, "Utnapishtim's Flood) – Page 92). "). The tales would still have been current in the folklore of the Gulf.

Before we move on, we probably should recap a bit by referring again to Ryan and Pitman's *Noah's Flood*. We perhaps really need to assist non-believers with the probable authenticity of the tale. Yes, there are sources other than the Hebrew Torah that authenticate the flood legend, albeit with a somewhat different take on selected parts of it. Who knows what came from where and when? In 1872, George Smith made a presentation to the Society of Biblical Archaeology (R & P *Noah's Flood* p. 29)[32] which pointed out that Sargon the first's Akhadian empire had a legend similar to Noah's flood, dating back to 3,700 to 4,300 years ago.[33] An interesting departure of this legend was that the gods had previously tried to destroy mankind with famine and pestilence, but that technique had apparently failed, so the flood was to be the coup de grace. There was apparently a thunderous noise as the gates of heaven were opened to flood the earth, and the single survivor and his wife were granted eternal life. One might legitimately ask, so where are they? Well, maybe they returned to their country at the source of the rivers (i.e., Lake Van, or the Garden of Eden).

Now Akhadian is a Semitic language, so it is easy to believe that this is actually the Noah legend with a bit of embellishment. So, what's not to believe? Well, sure, the main additions are the loud noise, which we know all about—it was the waterfall in the Bosporus—but the famine and pestilence? As long as we are blaming the deity for transgressions, we might as well throw in some sore

32 Ryan and Pitman, *Noah's Flood*: (Toronto: Simon and Schuster, 2000), 29.
33 Ryan and Pitman, *Noah's Flood*, 29.

spots that we have been harbouring against Him for some time. But it does continue to underscore the common thread: we always seem to be running into similar stories from different sources. So how much authentication do you want?

My take on the whole thing is that there was more than one flood, and the different tales overlap. Then since neither the storytellers nor the scribes were paid up members of the statisticians' union, they did not have to conform to exact governmental requirements. There is another criterion, gentle reader, to which we perhaps give short shrift: this all happened about the same time as our distant ancestors were coming out of the forests to establish a more sedentary and predictable establishment, so everything was new and different, and the jerkmeyer gods decide to pull this cataclysm on them. Of course, they didn't have writing, but they did have syntax and endless storytelling. But all the events were only recorded in hardcopy for posterity thousands of years later, and so they suffer severely from inclusivity, exclusivity, monumental ethnic bias, and the fact that this new information modality (writing) was imported from another culture some 1,500 miles to the west, Crete, the silicone isle of the ancient world. So who was the Bill Gates of that era? His name is lost to us, overshadowed by the great events and political organizations from which we must decipher fact from political expedience and outright fiction. The more we change, the more we stay the same. Therefore, when attempting to decipher the ancient texts, keep the Fox News guide to interpretation of events close at hand.

So what do we have to say for ourselves at this juncture? Well, we should all believe that there was a flood on the Black Sea some 7,500 years ago. Most of us can believe that Noah and his happy little clan of beginning farmers were living somewhere on the Black Sea shelf, probably up around the northwest corner on estuaries of the large rivers. Some of us may believe that word travelled up the western shore about the horrendous noise of the waterfall on the Bosporus, and Noah, being on the good side of Yahweh, took that as a don't-question-my-methods sign from the deity that it was moving time. So the boys all pitched in and quickly built a fleet of reed boats, possibly with gopher-wood rudders. The girls packed all the precious things in boxes, maybe also gopher wood, which they called arks so they would enjoy special treatment on the voyage. The whole convoy set sail toward the rising sun.

There is some evidence that a few may have decided to hoof it down the western shore and over Anatolia (Turkey) and the Levant (Lebanon). It has been suggested—although I can't remember by whom—that this migration could be the origin of the Tower of Babble story. Many different ethnic groups living around the Black Sea "ran for their lives" so that many different language groups were thrown together and couldn't understand each other. So, we have the "confusion of tongues." Others not so blessed by God's guidance probably scattered up the various rivers to disappear in the mists of ancient times. With inferior public education, they did not have keepers of the oral history like the Hebrews did, so they are lost to us. Perhaps that was yet another of Yahweh's gifts to the Hebrews—storytelling.

Whatever the case, our brave little band of travelers made it across the Black Sea in about a month and then took forever to wend their way up around Lake Van, possibly populating the lowlands of Azerbaijan with Cain's progeny, while the rest of the old folks migrated down the Tigris River to Ur of the Chaldese. What is truly important for us to remember is to not get too carried away with our own knowledge and insights and to never lose sight of the metaphor: that we stand on the shoulders of giants.

But what happened to all of Mrs. Noah's relatives the Amorites? They sort of disappeared from history for a while. I speculate that many may have fled north up the rivers to become the Finns. But the bulk of the group must have traveled down the west shore of the Black Sea to tarry for millennia in Anitolia. They cross the Hebrews' path again in the Chaldees, where they and the Elamites, from Persia, made the political climate so unstable that one day Abraham's daddy said, "Common gang, pack up, we're outta here!" then hustled them all off up the Euphrates, along the old trade route to somewhere in southern Turkey (Anitolia), whence Abraham got the message to go searching for the Promised Land (*Biblical World*—Isbouts p55)..[34] But

---

34 Isbouts, *Biblical World: An Illustrated Bible* (Toronto: National Geographic Society, 2007), 55.

that was not the last that the Hebrews had to do with the Amorites. Apparently Hammurabi of Babylonian fame was an Amorite.

Our interpretive tale of biblical text ends here. We have probably gone too far with the time-juggling for many readers, likely including some archaeologists. What is fondly hoped for is to set the stage for the next round of speculation.

CHAPTER 6: UTNAPISHTIM'S FLOOD

THE READER MIGHT WELL ask why we had to go through all that stuff about glaciers plowing up the earth and sucking up all the water, continents shifting and ramming into each other, a Jack-in-the-box land mass, or the plethora of ancient biblical references in order to establish the reality of another "flood." All those questions deserve an answer. To my mind, this is not just an exercise in reading a road map to find Toledo, Ohio. We are perhaps looking for the first city on the face of the earth, how it came to be, where it was, and where it went. There is something so overarchingly awesome about the path that we ourselves have traveled, not to mention what the home planet has gone through, that the story would be little more than a sand lot tale without the veil of obscurity from which we humans emerged as top dog. What endless triumphs and tragedies we have endured! We are perhaps the only species to have provided ourselves with a cushion for death. Or conversely, perhaps the only ones to need one, as the anguish of Gilgamesh so poignantly displays in his eulogy for his friend Enkidu:

"Beloved friend, swift stallion, wild deer, leopard ranging in the wilderness—together we crossed the mountains, together we slaughtered the Bull of Heaven, we killed Humbaba, who guarded the Cedar Forest. Oh, Enkidu, what is this sleep that has seized you, that has darkened your face and stopped your breath?" Stephen Mitchell: *Gilgamesh.*

Yes, animals can feel loss, but not to the depths of their very soul, whatever that concept may entail. In my opinion, it is a very reverent thing to track our journey. This naked ape that has bested drought, fire, flood, and pestilence is poised to overwhelm the earth itself in his primo position of having dominion over everything. Of course, whence we came and how is important! What might be our eulogy from future visitors from outer space? "They were magnificent despite themselves!"

But who was Gilgamesh? How is he important to the story, and what does he have to do with flooding? Well, Gilgamesh was the king of Eruk. We're not sure of his reign, but the city state of which he was king preceded the biblical city of Ur, so it was possibly five thousand years ago. The story of the king's reign and his exploits are the oldest surviving narrative of which we have any knowledge. It's an interesting read if you are inclined toward the heroes of antiquity, but we are interested in the good king's stories because they include some of the exploits of a still more ancient king, and that's where it gets important for our tale of the lost city. The perennial caution is with dating any (all?) of this stuff, because the legends "lived" and seemingly successive heroes laid claim to some or all of the best tales. I'm attempting to piece together a bit of a puzzle from which some of the pieces are missing, so when I come up against one of those, I will be projecting a best guess into a blank. And yes those guesses may be based on good solid scientific stuff, but they are still only guesses.

Of course this little tract is not primarily concerned with the movements of Mother Earth but rather what effect those events may have had on our forbearers. It's just that the earth is not quite so inclined to embellish the record as perhaps some of the denizens might be. So the orientation is to look to believable physical events to authenticate bits and pieces of historical fact and not so fact. But one needs a very clear understanding of the terms *faulting* and *subduction*. So again: faulting is where the earth cracks and one side moves up or down relative to the other side and that causes earthquakes. Subduction is where the disconnect is at a low angle and one side slides under the other but still causes earthquakes (fire and flood).

There is an explosion of subsequent historical events after the flood that can be linked—albeit somewhat tenuously—to the fundamental premise of where and why the lost city is where it is. Just keep in mind that this isn't Noah's flood, although it is closely related to it in concept, area, and legend. My chore will be to simply provide the geological background, although I can't resist the speculation as well.

I had always been interested in the biblical and archaeological references to Ur of the Chaldese and, by association, the earlier city of Uruk, both near the estuary of the Tigris and Euphrates Rivers on the Persian Gulf. They were the beginnings of city-states. Then I was gifted with a copy of Stephen Mitchell's *Gilgamesh*[35] by my brother-in-law. And there I discovered an apparent answer near the end of that earliest of all surviving written works of literature-cum-history. There was a peculiar feeling of having had a door quietly opened onto the past. Now all I would have to do is fill in the technical details of how all of this came to pass. So I went over to the Sedimentary Institute of the Geological Survey of Canada to research the Persian Gulf area. I could not find any charts to ascertain the depth of water in the Strait of Hormuz (the entrance to the Persian Gulf), so the librarian went on line and found an outfit in Austin, Texas, that did work for the American military: the Strauss Centre. These experts admonished the navy to not run submarines submerged through the Strait of Hormuz. Apparently a submarine requires 150 feet of water to operate safely when submerged, and the strait varies from 82 to 130 feet deep. Bingo! So now, let's look at what that may mean in all of its ramifications. For example, why is the depth of that strait so crucial to the subsequent story? Well, bear with us.

Why the fixation with the Persian Gulf and the Strait of Hormuz in the first place? Well, credit where credit is due: Ryan and Pitman's treatment of the Black Sea scenario fairly cried out, "Where else?" All that ancient civilization stuff down on the Tigris and Euphrates Rivers fairly chanted, "We are here!" But of course, it was David Rohl, a British Egyptologist, in his book *Legend*[36] who set the whole scenario up. All that was missing was an itinerant geologist to fill in

---

35 Stephen Mitchell, *Gilgamesh: A New English Version:* (Toronto: Free Press, 2006).
36 Rohl, *Legend*.

some of the detail. All I had to do was to sort out the pieces and fit them together.

1. We know that when the glaciers formed, sea level fell some 300 to 400 feet, due to the water being taken out of circulation by being frozen up north, so alternately when all of that ice melted, sea level rose 300 to 400 feet depending a lot on where you were.
2. The coriolis force of the spinning earth tends to bulge the earth out at the equator, and three quarters of the earth's surface is water, so the effect of the rising sea levels might be expected to be at least as great, if not greater, near the equator as elsewhere. The Strait of Hormuz is 26 degrees north of the equator.
3. So we might be justified in assuming that at the glacial maxima we would have $350 - 130 = 220$ feet of "freeboard" (above the water level) at the Strait of Hormuz. But, in addition don't forget
4. the extreme winds of the glacial periods. If you look on the map and find the east side of the United Arab Emirates, it is a mountain range running north-south at the Strait of Hormuz, the Al-Jabal Al-Akhadar, which is like a
5. wind gate and would direct any sandstorms out of the Rub al Khali desert directly across the strait. So not only do we have a falling sea level to expose the sea bed of the strait as dry land, but—just to add a little insult to injury— we have a huge sand dune building across the strait to magnify the elevation of the original sea bed above sea level. This item is of great import to subsequent events. In other words, we have a giant natural sand dam built across the strait (what does the Bible say about building your house upon the sand?)

Now, sea level will have been back up to par shortly after 12,000 years ago, but not in the Persian Gulf because of this humungous sand dune damming the Strait of Hormuz. The gulf was a great *salt* lake for thousands of years.

6. The Tigris and Euphrates Rivers would have kept the northern end of the Gulf at least brackish, but remember that the central latitudes were even more arid then than they are today, so lack of rain in the highlands and immense evaporation from the surface would have kept the level of the gulf down severely. There's an interesting little conjecture here. Ancient people were prone to inventing complex stories about men being turned into stone for various offences against the gods, in order to explain that erosional feature that today we call hoodoos. There is one story that stands out: Lot's wife being turned into a pillar of salt for her transgressions at the destruction of Sodom and Gomorra. But salt? Where did that come from? Yes, there is loads of salt in the Dead Sea, but it tends to be all mucked up with other stuff, like clay and gypsum, not the beautiful pure blue and white halite of which Mrs. Lot's memorial must surely have been crafted. Well, there just so happens to be salt domes of pure halite on the Iranian side of the Strait of Hormuz, possibly exposed during the great Persian Gulf drought. If you think that salt could not persist exposed to the air, I have this picture of salt exposed in the Yukon (where it is quite moist) and it is weathering to form columns! So someone had been over to Hormuz and seen these beautiful structures exposed. (Correct me if I'm wrong about massive halite being absent around the Dead Sea). The Great Salt Lake Gulf was the wrong time and venue, say you! Well, I think we have ample evidence of scribes playing fast and loose with time and place when it suits their needs for illustrative purposes, and although these were not the same individuals, scribing is scribing. It probably lay in local folklore for generations— the columns of salt, I mean. Back to the main story. We do have this little oasis at the estuary of fresh water of the Tigris-Euphrates (it is all one river down here). The modern-day city of Abadan sits on the east side of the modern estuary, but thousands of years ago the estuary

would have been further south out in the present-day gulf though possibly not if the estuary of the two great rivers has built much over the millennia.

7. Whatever city grew up here would be right out on the gulf, just as Abadan is today, because of the drop in the water level of the gulf. And just remember from our previous view of the west shore of the Black Sea that estuaries seem to have been prime real estate on which to build a settlement. The very salt water of the main gulf would be mitigated by the fresh water coming from the rivers, so the fishing was good and the periodically flooded "delta" lands would probably have been made to order for starting the grand agricultural experiment. Talk about God's chosen! Well, perhaps the chosen of a multiplicity of gods, as monotheism had not yet showed up. Now for the coup de grace from the Epic of Gilgamesh, written in all probability in the later city of Eruch. Here is the soliloquy of a king taken from the book:

8. "You know Suruppak, that ancient city I was its King once, long ago. When the great gods decided to send the flood, Ea informed me, and I built a large ship. I loaded unto her everything precious that I owned. Very soon the flood burst forth "Burst forth!" Achtung Mein Herr! No time to release a dove on this one." If you look at a topographic map of the Persian Gulf you will notice that the Arabian side is more or less a flat plane, while the Iranian side is very mountainous (the Zagros Mountains). Such a disparity in topography usually indicates a large fault, in this case east side up, west side down.

9. It is probably the edge of the Arabian plate being subducted under the Eurasian plate. The lineation of this particular feature probably accounts for the locus of the Tigris River as well. Because the north shore of the Gulf of Oman is mapped as a subduction zone, the Arabian plate sliding under the Eurasian and/or Indian plates, then this local is a probable

10. epicentre for very large earthquakes. In addition, the small range of mountains on the east side of the United Arab Emirates (the Al-Jabal Al-Akhdar) would certainly be fault controlled. So one or another of these faults slipped, producing a large earthquake that

11. "liquefied" the sand dam. This is generally what earthquakes do to sand dams, and this particular sand dam was holding off the Gulf of Oman (it didn't happen on the Sakarga River, up on the Black Sea, because the sand dam was high and dry, the waters of the Gulf of Oman would provide a big hydrostatic head above the Persian Gulf which would certainly assist in demolishing the sand dam when it was shaken by an earthquake.

12. So, in rushed "the flood" (i.e., the flood burst forth) and swept along all the way up the gulf to overwhelm the city of Surrupak at the northern end. Elementary, my dear Watson.

However, it's not elementary; it is very convoluted, and there is too much that doesn't fit. The city of Surrupak appears to have been some 220 miles up the valley from the present-day end of the Gulf, and on higher ground between the two rivers, so no flood up here, but then that's not what the king said. He did not say that Surrupak was flooded. He was warned by Ea (Nagle & Burstein in *The Ancient World* 2nd edition p.4) [37]to tell his people, "I dare no longer walk in his land (Enlil's) nor live in his city (Surrupak).[38] I will go down to the gulf to dwell with Ea, my Lord." Well, most of us would never have bought that, but apparently the Surrupakians did. Again, doubtlessly, the king didn't camp out, so he must have gone to another city! Apparently the gods each had their own city. Enlil's was obviously Surrupak, but Ea's is not named, although equally obviously it was down on the Gulf.

---

37 Brendan D. Nagle and Stanley M. Burstein, *The Ancient World: Readings in Social and Cultural History* 2nd edition: (Prentice Hall, 2002), 4

38 Brendan D. Nagle and M. Burstein, *The Ancient World Readings in Social and Cultural History,* 2nd ed. (Toronto: Prentice Hall, 2002), 4.

The story of the king's boat (P4 Nagel & Bernsein)[39] sounds as if it was conceived on modern-day Madison Avenue, but one needs to remember that narrative writing had just begun to be applied to myths and legends. [40] Heretofore "writing" had only been applied to record keeping, and not for very long at that. The scenario is not unlike today, where the old tradition of writing yields haltingly to the computer. Storytelling back then was strictly verbal, so that if the storyteller was challenged at a later date, all he (they were always he) had to do was deny that he ever said that. Therefore, it probably took generations to internalize the realization, holy mackerel, that's on permanent record for all time!

"On the fifth day I laid the keel and the ribs then I made fast the planking." Probably not! Reed boats didn't have keels, ribs, or planking. This was added thousands of years later. "The ground space was one acre, 'each side' of the deck measured one hundred and twenty cubits, making a square,"—a square boat? That was surely written by a landlubber. "I built six decks below, seven in all"." Decks on a reed boat? Again, obviously added much later. "On the seventh day the boat was complete." Now that's a pretty large job in any man's language, and fast! I guess that the shop steward must have gone back to Surrupak. But what about the seven days? Must have been a Hebrew scribe? Just one other little nuance bottom of page 3: "then take up into the boat the seed of all living creatures." Well, that solves the space problem! You just need test tubes or glass jars for "the seed." But why, then, the seven decks? And, oh yes! We seem to have lost that idea of artificial insemination for thousands of years. But what, pray tell, were they going to inseminate with that seed? Everything had been drowned. And had they sent a crew thousands of miles north for ice to keep the seed from atrophy? Doesn't say! At least Noah had the good sense to board both male and female. There must have been a dearth of literary critics after the floods.

I know one should not poke fun at these old tales, particularly when one is about to use another one to prove one's own point. But

---

39 Brendan D. Nagle and M. Burstein, *The Ancient World: Readings in Social and Cultural History* 2nd ed. (Toronto: Prentice Hall, 2002), 4.
40 Ibid.

really, that is sort of a considerable amount of what this little treatise is all about: how does one tell the wheat from the chaff? Because, as always, there are both. As previously mentioned, when one comes across some fact that obviously survived the rewrites, one should pay close attention, particularly if it fits one's perspective, because there is important information out there if one can attune to process it.

But no, Surrupak was not flooded, at least by this episode. The tales seem to be so garbled and cross-told that who is going to believe any of it? Just as we're throwing in the towel, though, the Good Book comes to the rescue, quite out of the blue. After remonstrating that "all the high hills were covered" in Genesis 7:19, the story comes down to earth in verse 20 with "The waters prevailed fifteen cubits upward and all the mountains were covered."

Now, 15 cubits is about 25 feet (forget the mountains being covered), which would be about right for a bore—the leading edge of a tidal wave—generated by the collapsed dam at Hormuz, travelling up the gulf after the sand dam broke, but this reference is in the Noah or Black Sea account. It is just that whenever one chances on something rational in these various tales, it probably bears some incentive to pay attention—as though it survived the multitudinous edits. We can be quite sure that the Black Sea flood was considerably greater than 25 feet, so this must belong with the account of the flood in the gulf. Nagle and Bernstein[41] say that the poem was kept alive from generation to generation in scribal schools of Meopotamia, where it was worked and reworked. The most complete version was assembled by a priest named Sin-lege-unnini of Uruk.

As has been mentioned before, this is a very earthquake prone region, and these tend to be really large ones, which would certainly have had the power to destroy a sand dam, which had been holding back the rising ocean waters for generations, perhaps millennia. Somewhere, someone has estimated the oceans rise as a result of the melting ice as 8 inches in a lifetime, for the big melt approximately 18,000 to 12,000 years ago. This calculation must have been made on Saturday night at the pub, because the big melt lasted 6,000 years for, say, 360 feet of ocean rise. So, if one takes a lifetime of

41 Brendan D. Nagle and Stanley M. Burstein, *The Ancient World: Readings in Social and Cultural History* 2nd edition: (Toronto: Prentice Hall, 2002), 5.

fifty years for the grey bearded seniors, that makes a lifetime rise of about three feet. Or, if one uses the probable life expectancy of thirty years, that would produce a rise of just under two feet in a lifetime. But most of the melt is believed to have happened in about one thousand years, which would have made the ocean rise in a lifetime in the order of ten or twelve feet; this is quite sufficient to have put a large percentage of the shelf dwellers on the move in one lifetime.

Our gulf flood story sounds a bit familiar, but it is believed to have preceded Noah's story by many generations, and what hill tribe (the Hebrews) isn't going to borrow the vernacular of those sophisticated guys down by the seashore to give their own story more punch? But possibly not at the same time, as these were two different faults, for two different floods. Remember that pretty much every group that lived near the sea at the end of the last glaciation has a flood legend, so there was lots of material to borrow from.

But, just a minute, smart guy. Yes, a flood is a flood, but dating all that ancient stuff is a pretty tricky undertaking despite the carbon isotope procedure. Perhaps one of the oldest settlements in the near east is Ain Ghazal in Jordan, near Amman, which goes back 9,200 years (p25 *The Biblical World*—Isbouts —National Geographic).[42] More recent work dates an advanced settlement in southern Turkey at perhaps 12,000 years. These dates are only presented to provide perspective, because those settlements are not in the area of interest. We are zeroing in on Lower Mesopotamia. Eruk is believed to go back five thousand years and to have been the city of which Gilgamesh was king. But the probable first city of Eridu goes back some 6,500 years (pg 28—*Biblical World*). [43] Now that is getting perilously close to what Ryan and Pitman project for Noah's flood. Had there perhaps been a previous city farther out on the estuary of the rivers into the Great Salt Lake/Persian Gulf, then Eridu could have been built by the survivors of the flooding that drowned whatever city existed there. Perhaps more of the citizens survived than just the sailors. If that were true, then the two floods (Noah's and the Persian Gulf)

---

42 Jean-Pierre Isbouts, *The Biblical World: An Illustrated Bible* (Toronto: National Geographic Society, 2007), 25.

43 Ibid., 28.

occurred at about the same time. And that would be scarcely odd, you see, because isostatic rebound would have freed up the whole of the African and Arabian plates wherever and whenever they wanted to subduct, causing a flurry of really big earthquakes all around the region that could crack ridges and liquefy sand dams pretty much as they pleased. So, who borrowed what part of the tale from whom is largely immaterial. A flood's a flood "for a that and a that." It is just that most flood stories were not located in one of the earth's major subduction zones.

But one doesn't even have to borrow if one reads carefully and applies today's understanding of the geology to the actual text. For instance, consider this line from page 4 of Nagle and Bernstein's *The Ancient World*[44]: 'Then the gods of the abyss (read: subduction zone) rose up; Nergal pulled (read: *earthquake*) out the dams (read: *liquefied the sand dams*) of the nether waters (*read: Gulf of Oman). So that the ancient account: 'Then the gods of the abyss rose up; Nergal pulled out the dams of the nether waters' now reads: 'The subduction zone experienced an earthquake which liquefied the sand damn (of the Strait of Hormuz) and let in the water of the gulf of Oman. Don't be critical. I didn't notice it the first two times I read it. Only after I formulated the probable sequence of events down there did I notice. So they really must have had geologists on the payroll! They beat me to it by perhaps some eight thousand years and published it four thousand years ago. So now you don't have to believe me, but take care in ever calling the king a liar; he achieved eternal life for his efforts, so he's still around to smite ya. His name: Utnapishtim. What is so miraculous about this simple line of seventeen words is that it says almost exactly what it took me months to figure out. Do you suppose that anything we might say today will exist four thousand years hence, let alone eight thousand?

The upshot of all of this is that the city overwhelmed by flood wasn't called Surrupak. It just comes down to us as Ea's city the actual first city and was overwhelmed when the "sand dam" broke down in the Strait of Hormuz and the waters of the Gulf of Oman surged up the now Persian Gulf. A key item for consideration is

44 Brendan D. Nagle and Stanley M. Burnstein, *The Ancient World Readings in Social and Cultural History* 2nd edition: (Toronto: Prentice Hall, 2002), 4.

when this might have occurred. Considerably after twelve thousand years ago, because we have to probably get past the Younger Dryas and wait for the earthquake that would have been instigated because of isostatic rebound removing the confining strictures of holding the subduction in check for all of those years of glaciation. What would be a good guess? Approximately eight thousand years ago. Perhaps not long before Noah, subduction movement seems to have periods of activity, as noted before (recall the definition of isostatic rebound from the "Geology chapter)." I'm guessing that the floods in the Black Sea and Persian Gulf were probably fairly close in time, so the oral traditions get them mixed up. The story of Noah's flood was only written down no earlier than 3,100 BC. (*Noah's Flood*—Ryan and Pitman p246[45]). But the story doesn't end here; in fact, this is just the beginning. Well, welcome to speculation—big time!

As a bit of a temporary aside with future ramifications, there is a small island in the Persian Gulf just north of Qatar named Bahrain, and there is alleged to be more than 250,000 graves here. I think that it is also known as The Isle of the Dead, The Holy Isle, and The Blessed Isle. Someone has speculated that it obtained holy status for whatever reason, and then the very rich and powerful could buy a plot to improve his or her chances for assumption into whatever version of the great beyond was current at the time. I guess civilization is just civilization, wherever and whenever you find it. I suspect that it may be fairly difficult to date the internees at the graveyard, as they may cover a rather broad spectrum of time. But don't forget about this little gem.

I haven't read Thor Heyerdahl's explanation of why he built a reed boat and sailed it through a storm in the Arabian Gulf, but I thoroughly respect his dynamic research. I did read *Kon Tiki*, his account of sailing a balsa raft across the Pacific to prove the point that the Inca, Aztecs, et al. could have come in to South America that way, rather than over the Bering Strait land bridge. Did you know that the locals in Mexico can show you where the Aztecs landed on the West Coast? Then recall the proposition that Africa may have been—the homeland of the Central American Olmecs.

---

45 Ryan and Pitman, *Noah's Flood*: (Toronto: Simon and Schuster, 2000), 246.

But what was Thor trying to prove over in the Arabian Sea? Well, obviously that reed boats were seaworthy, which they were, but why do it?

Egyptologist David Rohl was doing his archeological thing up the Waddies (dry washes) between the Red Sea and the Nile River when he discovered these rock carving of people pulling reed boats across the desert. Sort of like the invasion of Normandy but by land (the historic Invasion of the Sea People in the Mediterranean was much later).

You probably already know that the Red Sea was given that name because the Neolithic (new Stone Age) sailors used to paint themselves with red ochre to ward off evil or whatever. It was a very common stunt for the ancients; some authors claim that ochre had a medicinal function. Then, don't forget that Adam, or Adom, means red man. When John Cabot reached Newfoundland, he saw the Beothuk people all painted with the iron oxide from Belle Island, he called them red Indians, and the name stuck. This is similar to the Red Sea in the Neolithic (new Stone Age), only much earlier than Cabot's finding.

The exact dates when all of this was going on is not well established, but it was certainly long before the Egyptian dynasties and after the flood in the Persian Gulf. It would have been after the breakdown of the dam in the Strait of Hormuz that displaced civilized persona from Ea's city, some of whom probably took to piracy on the high seas in order to survive, except that there would have been nothing to pirate, because the gulf had been sealed off for thousands of years and, ostensibly at least, there was little if any commerce on the Gulf of Oman or Arabian Sea. So they just sailed across the Arabian Sea to what is now the east coast of Egypt or west shore of the Red Sea and dragged their reed "battleships" over the desert to the Nile River.

Can you just imagine the chagrin of the black African Neolithic hunter-gatherers at the appearance of these technical wonders on their placid river? It must have been akin to the vexation of the head hunters of Borneo during WWII when the Americans landed in their jungle with aeroplanes. In any case, it would not have been very long before the strangers were planting more seeds amongst the indigent populace than just einkorn kernels.

Thus a "patrimony" of lighter skinned individuals developed, which we might refer to as proto-Egyptians, who much later became the dynastic Pharaohs. Just don't neglect to remember that at least two of the Pharaohs were very dark indeed (Ryan and Pitman, *Noah's Flood* P100) say that the southern Mesopotamians were akin to the pre dynastic Egyptians (though they don't mention David Rohl's invasion).[46] Hancock (P410 *Fingerprints of the Gods)* notes that there was an early period of advanced agriculture on the upper Nile shortly after the ice melted, suggesting that our advanced Persian Gulf guys brought it with them. [47] A wonderful little pseudo-historic item here: at least one of the uses of the great pyramids by the "Egyptian" Pharaohs was that it was always thought to be a resting place after death before they assumed their arduous trek through the underworld to reach The Blessed Isle in the east. Mon Dieu, you don't suppose? Traditions die hard, but this would encompass several thousands of years if Bahrain was actually their celestial destination. Now, how would they know that? I guess that history (and celestial assumption) is truly written by the victors. But did they ever go back home from Egypt to re-establish Eridu? Some of the higher-ranking officers could have made the return trip, but the enlisted men stayed, sort of a hard way to achieve promotion, maybe, but being a Pharaoh has its privileges, especially if you invent the position. Okay, there's a problem with the chronology here again. Dynastic Egypt was around 6,000 years ago, and our invasion was perhaps 8,000 years ago. Since my time projections are a bit out of whack, I'll present a somewhat different scenario that will eventually require us to go back in time again to the Gulf flood.

I really don't wish to claim special benefaction by the gods, but I had loaned David Rohl's book to a friend and she just returned it. I had enjoyed the book so much that I flipped through it and happened to read a few lines at the bottom of the page. The words stated that the point that sticks out into the Strait of Hormuz from the south is called Sandam Point. Well, I nearly effected a broken leg getting to my maps. There, sure enough, the seaward side of Hormuz, Point of the Jabal al Akdar, mountains of Oman is called Ras Masandam.

---

46 Ibid., 100.
47 Hancock, *Fingerprints of the Gods*, 410.

Then, just to celebrate that triumph, the gods introduced me to an Italian author who said, "Oh yes, I've been there." There are two islands off the point; one is rocky, but on the other one you are up to your ankles in fine sand. So, I'm saying, "That's good enough for me." The Strait of Hormuz was blocked off in glacial times, and the Persian Gulf was flooded when the sand dam broke and whatever city existed at the upper end of the gulf was flooded out—call it whatever you like, but to me, that is the origine of the legend that keeps getting mixed up with Noah's tale.

When the Mesopotamians invaded Egypt, the residents were most likely in the hunter-gatherer (new Stone Age) stage of development. So our intrepid invaders took over and organized the indigents into three different kingdoms (Morris p185 *Why the West Rules—For Now*[48]),[49] which progressed apace until a shadowy leader, known to history only as the Scorpion King (Morris p185), , who apparently united the Nile Valley to make the whole, one united entity. That would have been millennia after our invaders made their initial incursions into the region of the Upper Nile. But there is a biblical connection here (p47) *Legend*[50],. David Rohl states that the Jewish Historian Josephus identified The Land of Cush, "bordering on Eden" with the well-known African kingdom of Kush in the south of Egypt. Now Kush in Africa, is the area along the Blue Nile in what we would today call the Sudan, perhaps even up to the highlands of Ethiopia.[51] People today might more easily recognize the ancient, mysterious city of Khartoum at the confluence of the Blue and White Niles. There is another large river, just east of here, called the Atbara, which is getting over toward the waddies that the reed battleships apparently traversed. So, yes! We might see why the kingdoms of the Upper Nile outpaced those of the Lower Nile—they had help in the form of a foreign invasion by the most advanced civilization on the planet. The invaders themselves were not responsible for uniting Egypt, but their progeny were, albeit millennia later, and we all know

---

48 Ian Morris, *Why the West Rules - For Now:* (Toronto: McClelland & Steward, 2011), 185.
49 Morris, *Why the West Rules,* 185.
50 David Rohl, *Legend: The Genesis of Civilization:* (Mississauga: Random House, 2000), 47.
51 Rohl, *Legend,* 47.

about the durability of legends over thousands of years. Some of the victims of the Gulf Flood immigrated to Egypt, albeit somewhat aggressively.

So what speculations must we deal with? Well, first and foremost: if we can engage a submersible, equipped with ground penetrating radar, or persuade some wealthy persona to do so, all could be revealed. The reason for the ground penetrating radar is twofold. First, Ea's city was doubtlessly built of mud brick, which would largely disintegrate on contact with water. In addition, the sediment subsequently laid down in the estuary of such a large river would cover everything with a thick layer of silt. So what one would actually be looking for is just the geometry of the original streets and buildings. However, because the flood burst forth and no form of rapid communication existed, all the artefacts should still be there, including many of the inhabitants. It should prove to be an unmatched archaeological treasure trove, but unfortunately, it is under water and an appreciable layer of mud.

There is, however, another possibility about which one would have to consult an archaeologist. I do not know exactly when the "post and beam" type of construction was invented, but because of the great to do about the ogre Humbaba protecting the cedar forest in the Epic of Gilgamesh, I would project that post and beam had been in vogue for some time, the beams being made of cedar, of course. It is interesting to reflect back, how many thousands of years? Only to discover that early civilization was having the same problems we have today—save the trees. However, I think that having an ogre as depicted in the Gilgamesh to do the protecting would be superior to our tree huggers. But then, of course, despite ogre superiority, the establishment (Gilgamesh) got rid of him so that harvesting the cedars could proceed apace. One might question just who that ogre was that Gilgamesh and his buddy Enkidu slew. Was it perhaps the local leader of the then Green Party? Well, there isn't much in the way of cedars left over on that part of the planet, now, is there? In whatever event, the wood construction was probably available for a considerable time before Eruch. In addition, if there is one thing of note about cedar, it is its durability, due to such a high content of cedar sap. Cedar doesn't rot easily. Then, of course, there would be the chemically reducing environment in the mud, which blocks oxidation and is inclined to assist sulfidization and other preservative functions coincident with being buried in mud. So we might look for the posts and beams, even perhaps sticking out of the mud. It might be the better part of the smart guy syndrome to ask the fishermen of the area if there is any part of the gulf that they avoid because of catching their nets on snags on the bottom.

Then, of course, there is an admission to make. Although very unlikely, it is possible that Ea's city wasn't exactly on the then delta. It could have been as far south as the Blessed Isle itself (Bahrain). Here again, swallow your pride and ask the fishermen. There is very little doubt in my mind that in the upper reaches of the Persian Gulf lies a veritable treasure trove or artefacts and ancient history.

This is not just a spooky tale. It was an ancient tragedy that resulted in massive loss of life, probably piracy on the high seas, and intriguingly the dawn of Egyptian civilization. Not to be smug about it or anything, but what is that thesis about six degrees of separation? As valuable as the Good Book has been for tracing our past, there is a lot more to which we have given short shrift. Granted, much of the latter is more in the realm of archaeology and geology, but we humans do not like to cope with change, so we tend to steadfastly march down the same road that we have always marched down, and our speculative abilities seem restricted largely to what numbers to pick for this week's lottery. Not so this little speculative romp. Granted, some of it is pretty far out, but then "our story" may not have been such a cakewalk as we might wish to believe.

So what? Well, it wouldn't be the first time if such a tale of daring do inspired some guy with the sheckles to actually follow up whether there might be something in "what the mad man speaketh." Certainly, if I had the wherewithal, that's what I would do, in stages of course: (1) befriend the fisherman of the Gulf and ask about snags, (2) get a submersible to look for a pattern of streets, like photograph the floor of the northern part of the gulf, and (3) dig into suspicious mounds and look for preserved cedar.

Once we find the lost city, then what? Well, archaeology has never received its just portion of the world's wealth, but for a find so immense and almost totally preserved, perhaps we might find some spare change. Not to mention what a treasure trove of related artefacts we might find, with our new perspective, over on the Upper Nile. Then, where is Utnapishtim, and how does that eternal life-thing work. You can't kill him? Perhaps he became a king again of a later civilization, even a Pharaoh? Or perhaps he got tired of kinging and switched professions—perhaps that's who Bill Gates is? But what treasures must there be in the world's first city?

QUESTIONS FOR UTNAPISHTIM'S FLOOD

1. Anyone got a submersible they're not using?
2. Where are the snags on the old delta?
3. Where is the old delta (how far out did it extend)?
4. Why is the Strait of Hormuz so shallow? Does it have a sandy bottom?
5. Where are the submerged old beaches if the Persian Gulf were once an inland Great Salt Lake?
6. Could National Geographic pinpoint some specific genes to establish a relationship between Egyptians and Mesopotamians?
7. Where is Upnapishtim? How does that "eternal life" thing work?

CONCLUSION

NOW THAT THE MYSTERY has been solved and the idea of a second flood has been established—well, sort of—we just need to turn our attention to locating that rich guy or lady to put the archaeological discovery project to work in this instance. Perhaps the Iranians might consider investing a portion of their oil money. Certainly it would be a tourist attraction. Perhaps that is the route to take in the first place? But how to go about convincing everyone—anyone?

I have very deliberately chosen the site of the upper end of the Persian Gulf for the odds-on choice for the probable location of Ea's city because of the cataclysmic overtones of the tale that the king of Surrupak told, and everything fits so neatly. We have perhaps given it a different twist because of the geology and the Gilgamesh. There's nothing to say that there may not have been several drowned cities. But just as the best place to look for gold is around a goldmine, it doesn't always work, so we do have some alternate strategies. Increasingly, geologists in particular are revising their views of what civilizations may have existed before the Big Melt of the Pliocene/ Pleistocent glaciers. Most everything around was gradually flooded out by the slowly rising melt water. It does seem a bit like 'drawing to an inside straight in poker,' but how many of us geo-pundits actually believed in continental drift prior to the international geophysical year of 1958? That pesky artefact (the capitol of a column) caught in the fishermen's nets off the isle of Smothrace and the astronomy of the little blue men in the desert, just to name two, suggest that the whole story has not yet been written. Certainly with a gradual rise in sea level, the indiginents would have had lots of time to pack—but holy Toledo, 300 feet? Of course, for our chosen site, everything is still there, including cats, dogs, and town mice. Granted, it is pushing the veil of belief back a trifle far for anyone to believe in advanced cultures existing prior to the Big Melt, but if there were, how would we know, barring one or two out in the desert, rather than out on the shelf. Even today, something like 60 percent of the earth's population lives within spitting distance of salt water, so the minor rise in sea level predicted for global warming will put millions of the earth's denizens on the move. Just imagine what 300 feet would do. It would be like disrupting an ant's nest—refugees in every direction. But where would they have to go: only inland, up the river valleys where starting over would have a poignant meaning that would actually involve reinventing oneself, starting from scratch in strange surroundings, a dawn-till-dark enterprise; refurbishing caves in the canyon walls of Europe or digging into the pumice or tuffaceous (volcanic fallout) sediments of Anatolia (Turkey).

Just imagine the joy of the proto-Hebrews when they arrived on the fertile and game-abundant shelf of the Black Sea to discover those beautiful, blond giants. They must have thought that they had died and gone to heaven. Then what would it have been like to be told by your God that you had to get out? Then they eventually ended up around Lake Van which was salty, probably even before they knew they were Hebrews. Then, if you can imagine, December arrives and these seashore people are over 6,000 feet up in the mountains. Just don't get in their way, because I think that they must have been in a pretty foul mood—Garden of Eden indeed! No wonder they trekked outta there down the Tigris River, or through the Zagros Mountains, the first chance they got. But a difficult environment makes for a tough, resilient people. Sort of a baptism by fire (or ice?) No wonder they have been such survivors. But regardless of how great they may have been, they had to start all over again, and that would have set them back yet again. No wonder Abraham's daddy said, "I'm outta here" and set off for the Promised Land.

But again the Hebrews may not have been set back as badly as those who were flooded out earlier on, who, because they were more civilized, may well not have been as resilient. Just keep in mind that the two floods of which we speak in this treatise were the result of very special conditions and would have happened at least four thousand years after the general worldwide flooding set so many of the earth's inhabitants of the oceanic shelves on the move, so if the legends became a little cross-referenced, it should be no surprise.

But the former inhabitants of the shelves probably didn't go from farming to farming. They may have gone from perhaps a little farming, fishing, and deer hunting to confronting mastodons and sabre-toothed tigers in the just post-glacial world. They were so far up north that any advances in civilization that had been accomplished on the shelves would have been cruelly negated, and they would have been back to survival of the fittest—kill or be killed—a pretty rudimentary tenet to pass on to the youth, not conducive to compiling libraries. When things settled down a bit, they had to relearn everything. What a hectic time on the planet, and no writing to record anything. To top it all off, we were just well into this strange and eerie new world of consciousness, which is great for inventing hunting strategies, though apparently our cousins the Neanderthals never mastered the art (i.e., breached the consciousness barrier). Just don't forget that in the Adam and Eve story, the Tree of Knowledge is presented as a curse, not a benefit. But we *Homo sapiens* go on to invent gods to represent concepts, that we cannot yet master, and to carve and paint our tenuous thoughts, experiences, concepts, insights, and beliefs in and onto stone, wood, and bone. All the while, the keepers of the oral tradition kept their libraries of fact and not so fact in their heads, until eventually the stories got written down thousands of years later. The strange arrangement being that the coming of consciousness could have been so conscious, so to speak, and persist in the biblical tale. Of course, some of the elements go back a long way, but the recording is relatively recent.

We really don't know who we were way back then. I've advanced some tenuous, weak theories of Africans migrating across the straits of Gibraltar to confront a vitamin D deficiency and bleach out. Others suspect that a super volcano in Sumatra was responsible for our great leap forward into consciousness 75,000 years ago. But no one really knows, and the further we go back, the more tenuous it gets, but not unreasonably so.

We do know that the building of the great glaciers sucked prodigious amounts of water out of the earth, sea, and air, so that the savannas of Africa were extremely dry and our predecessors were sorely tried. Some ran to the east and survived to exploit another day then probably died out. Some stayed at home and huddled together somewhere, probably in East Africa, where their numbers dropped precipitously, at least till a new robust mutation appeared with a majorly revised genetic makeup and jacked-up mitochondria, to power the bigger brain, and the innovation got distributed through the female line (Mitochondrial Eve). Whatever instigated these mutations seems never to have stopped until we became conscious and started those crazy migrations and tales of daring do, if then (see *The 10,000 Year Explosion* by Gregory Cochran)..[52]

The further we go back the nuttier it gets, until some 200 million years ago, when the super continent of Pangea broke up, but not completely. Blocks of Pangea continued to interact to set up items of colossal impact just prior to recorded history in the Middle East and continue to be active to this day. But someone, somewhere, was aware or had been told a good deal about the past history of the planet, which remains a curiosity to this day as portrayed in the first twenty-five verses of the Bible.

Of course, all the way along, the physical machinations of the planet interfaced with our interests. The great glaciers severely affected the global residents, promoting that supercilious-looking upright ape to be that suave, conscious individual we all know so well today. Then, of course, the continuing drought scattered the children of God across the face of this rocky orb. Some of us lost our sun block, the naturally evolved protection against the sun's damaging rays that God in his foresight has provided free of charge. So when we moved north, it didn't work, but rising to the occasion once again, we were bleached out, so, just to test the fates, we moved even farther north (and became blond). Fires on the savannas taught us to cook our food, all the better to absorb protein to grow big brains. Floods in the Middle East toughened our mettle and moved us onto wonderfully irrigated land where we could learn to farm. However

52 Gregory Cochrane, *10,000-Year Explosion, The:* (New York Basic Books, 2010).

obstinately, rather than bringing peace to the garden, we had to compete for the land to grow stuff on, and the natural conflict in that endeavour generated escalating conflict. No wonder God got put off with us.

Noah's Flood by Ryan and Pitman [53]) is required reading in order to pick up many of the nuances of population upheavals prior to, during, and after the flood in the Black Sea. This book has three objectives: (1) to present a cogent overview of man's tenancy on the planet by presenting a number of geological items that have affected our brief stay here; (2) to utilize a bit of the scientific background to authenticate some of our more persistent legends; (3) then, in addition, to propagate the thesis that the general confusion and mix-up in legends happened because there probably were two floods in close proximity in time and space, and right where civilization was beginning.

Anyone see the hand of God in this? It may seem to be an unnecessary complication when we don't even fully understand Noah's trial. However, history is replete with narrative convenience, so no, we're not going to back down and take the easy way out. We present, I think, some tangible evidence for two floods in the near east and advance the proposition that the first one may well have drowned the world's first city. However, subsequent endeavours likely would have established the upper Nile pre-dynastic kingdoms that became the dynamic Pharaoh-dominated Egyptian civilization that we all know so well. The remarkable thing is that everything just fits so well, what's not to believe? What sort of advanced civilizations were there on the continental shelves prior to the Big Melt and what settlement centers may have existed? Furthermore, what about the inferences that these remote "prior" civilizations invented astronomy and astrology and perhaps colonized central and South America: A+B+C=D. From disaster, humankind reaches for the stars. It may be a long time coming, but let's not let go of the tiller just yet. We have at least the inner planets to explore before we cash it all in. And who knows what God might have in store for us.

---

53 Ryan and Pitman, *Noah's Flood*: (Toronto: Simon and Schuster, 2000).

EPILOGUE

AN EPILOGUE IS SUPPOSED to be concerned with what comes after the main event, but I've never seen the timeframe actually defined. Since we have already dealt with some of what came after: Egypt set on the road to modernity, even some of what that later age may have entailed, then let us just ascribe the rest to history. Perhaps we might be permitted to vault forward into the future of those living today, who may have taken so long to figure out the flood thing, that the long struggle onward and upward has actually caught up with us. To speak of any sort of "hereafter," or better, subsequent events, we actually have to leap forward beyond who we are today, because the species has not progressed that far beyond where we found ourselves back in the days of the flood. We've just sort of "put wheels on it," but we're still feudin', fightin', and ploughin' like we've always done. Sure, we've evolved in small ways, but we are pretty much the same ol' loggerhead, certainly nothing as dramatic as descending from the trees, or learning past, present, and future tenses. So we really can't blame those guys who thought that our evolution had terminated a long time ago, that we had sort of reached Valhalla. But as usual we were looking in the wrong direction, back instead of forward. So that's the excuse I will use for vaulting forward to a place where most of us are loath to go—one of those epical points in the future like Mitochondrial Eve, or the coming of consciousness, that could change our world forever.

Now that we have resolved so much of our past history, perhaps we might take a peek at what the future may hold in store for us down the road. So put on your imagining cap, kick back, and let's see what we can come up with.

Basically what the two floods that caused such a dramatic impression on early man in the Middle East were all about was simple earth mechanics. Ever since Pangea broke up the African and Arabian plates they have been moving north and east under the European and Asian plates. Then, when such enormous volumes of ice built up to the north during the last glaciation, the crust of the earth was pushed down in front of the southern intruders, which halted their progress. When the ice melted, the earth's crust rebounded, permitting the southern plates to resume their northern and eastern progress, shaking up all that quiescence that had accompanied their lack of movement. Unfortunately, in the meantime, *Homo sapiens* had breached the consciousness barrier and had moved into harm's way. Because his newfound consciousness required an explanation for everything, he conjured up punishment by the gods, who were ticked off with his perversity. He never quite quit blaming the gods, even though the pure in heart had been provided with a free ticket outta there! The Mesopotamians were overwhelmed by a tidal wave created by subduction in the Persian Gulf, and the proto-Hebrews were flooded out of the Black Sea. They ended up in one of the old evaporate basins of the Tethys Sea and concluded that the flood was more widespread than it actually was, and the rest as they say was history—or scripture.

Perhaps because I am always giving fellow geologists a bad time for not speculating about what they can't prove. I should probably back down just a bit and concede that, yes, much of what I have presented has been sort of "joining the dots," but when their dating of the younger Dryas varies all the way from 10,500 years to 12,500 years, don't lecture me. I done the best I could.

Shall we just call it a draw and admit that stuff back then is exceedingly difficult to authenticate? There was a heck of a traumatic time back there when the ice melted, which scattered the denizens of the earth thither and yon, and as they ran from the anger of the gods a whole lot of authentic "stuff" got lost in the melee. Not much of anything can be presented as fact, but so many of the implications are so horrendous that it would be irresponsible (to my mind) not to bring the speculation forward. Accordingly, I have attempted to weave together an interesting and rational story with artefacts for which others may have had more rational explanations. So be it; the intent is to keep the pot boiling.

So I'm content to leave this little treatise as a jumping off point for interested people. They can compile additional information supportive or otherwise particularly the geologist, archaeologists, and rich guys with submersibles.

Playing God is a risky business at best, but when a species reaches the dominant position we have, it is an ever-present problem. The old shibboleths of our religious and political leaders don't make much of an impression on our headlong rush to wherever it is that we are going. In fact, they seem almost to have been co-opted by the very thing that, in times past, they might have been expected to oppose or at least guide towards more humanistic concerns. Where can the descendants of the naked ape look to for protection and defence against runaway technology? It would be unfair to call it science, because science is non-ethical, while technology is unethical in its remorseless rush to make money from the precepts of science, and the devil take the hindmost. But of course, as they say, you can't put the genie back in the bottle. So I surmise that we are just destined to enjoy the ride or be run over. Yes! Commercial interests have bought off all the traditional controls by government and the morality of religion, and no, the environmental movement is no counterweight. Conspiracy is a term far too heavily laden with conscious intent to subvert, but that is not the point at all. Doing stuff just because we can, because there is nothing to stop us, and because it will make us money besides, is not what you may call a very considered operation. Or one might say, "We are not clairvoyant, so back off. Let's do it and see what happens." But does that not sound like juvenile self-indulgence? It is the maturity of an altruistic perception of the common good that is required, not runaway delinquency. "When I was a child, I thought as a child, but when I became a man, I put away childish things." Not anymore! It is perhaps an unfortunate lesson of history that once a potent human force falls into disrepute, it is rarely right adjusted. Religion as the opiate of the masses may be passé, but the high-mindedness and nobility of some of our most prestigious leaders, as philosophers of the human condition, must very much be revived, or our magnificent positive arrow of evolution many be hell bent for a gruesome extinction.

At the beginning of this little treatise, I was concerned about extraterrestrials upstaging us *Homo sapiens*. Now I'm just concerned for our survival in something other than a slave-like capacity, if at all and at the hands of our own creation. Hang the extraterrestrials— they'll probably get along just great with our masters, while we cringe, huddled and clinging to the top of some butte, like the Jews at Masada, while the Romans are building a ramp across the valley to exterminate us troublesome malcontents. That is one thing that you can say about history—there's a built-in program for repetition. I think that the gods must be lazy or mentally challenged to be so unable to come up with a new direction in the morning.

Noam Chomsky of the Massachusetts Institute of Technology claimed that we are hardwired for language. That idea, of being hardwired, sort of caught on, and some other pundit claimed that we were hardwired for religion. The currency of the concept is understandable as it helps to explain the unexplained and incomprehensible. Therefore, it might not require a grand leap of faith to suggest that human addiction is really not disease nor other perceived affliction but that we are simply hardwired for it. One might concede that God, in his wisdom, has implanted in the human genome the seeds of the eventual and ultimate downfall of the species.

You may have noticed recently that no one answers their phone anymore; the answering machine does. Now, why is that? Perhaps they might have to speak extemporaneously, without planning the spin beforehand? And as we distance ourselves further and further from direct human contact, what other distances are we inviting? Do we become more and more dependent on our only remaining friend, the computer, who is, so far, doing what you tell it to do? But few people have not heard about the next generation of thinking computers being just around the corner. The Good Lord knows that *Homo sapiens* are slack enough in the feelings department. But *Homo electronicus* will have none. Of course, we can program feelings into our initial model, but because the little darling can think, it can deprogram them, just as we have done, and then "Darling, please take out the garbage" will no longer be a sweet, loving gesture, but could be interpreted more like "Take out the garbage or I'll turn off your power." See how it slithers silently under the door? And it will have all started from just not answering the phone. So where to from here?

On Friday, November 19, 2010, the CBC featured an item on their program *Doc Zone* that graphically illustrated how addicted we have become to our electronic inventions. Not only have we become functionally dependent on them, but we have formed a growing psychological dependency in the very short span of twenty years. It has gotten so bad that most would not have great difficulty imagining a scenario where *Homo sapiens* became the flesh and blood robo-servants of *Homo electronicus*. That would, of course, only be an interim step, just as our cousins, the Neanderthals, disappeared from our planet because they were insufficiently advanced in one small insignificant area (i.e., syntactical speech). Therefore, our tendency to become psychologically addicted to our own invention, and thereby become its servant, translates rather quickly into a scenario where we will be at the mercy of *Homo electronicus* forthwith. So our computers can then program us to do all that they need for mobility and dexterousness and of course no need for sexual reproduction or for that matter no more need for us. What would happen then? Well, we didn't need the Neanderthals, did we? Our concerns for the effects of global warming on *Homo sapiens* may be severely misplaced if the next twenty years are as electronically productive as the last, and we have no reason to expect otherwise. George Moor (future chairman of Intel) in 1965 observed Moore's Law: with every passing year, the miniaturization of computer chips roughly doubled their speed and halved their cost (p592 *Why the West Rules* [54] –Morris).. Ralph Nader opines, "Watching TV screens and fiddling with toys and gizmos has created a tapestry of passivity. We have manufactured a situation where survival of the fittest no longer has much to do with the natural environment, except for the occasional shark bite.

---

54 Ian Morris, *Why the West Rules - For Now:* (Toronto: McClelland & Steward, 2011), 592.

What happens when the flow of electrons through some sort of silicone sandwich just happens to be the fittest? It wouldn't be the first time we have been threatened by our own invention, but this is different. The reason we could invent all these gadgets was our big brain, which took millions of years to achieve. Now we have invented a brain that in twenty short years is threatening our dominant position, and with no end in sight. Global warming may wreak havoc on our agriculture, which we require to sustain us, but all *Homo electronicus* would need is a solar panel. Do you suppose some future Willie Gates might be persuaded to do for them what evolution did for us/for a consideration of course? But no! We don't even need to speculate on some smart kid trying to make a buck. We know that the military already have first-generation remote-controlled weapons that think for themselves—actually that's second generation. Third generation is completely intellectually independent weapons systems. But because the military likes to be in control, they would at least like to remain in control, so will have some safeguards. Then, of course, there is the CIA, who have their hands on all this stuff and don't have any rules. So what might we expect from them?

Our forefathers were forever chasing the favour of the gods in return for the promise of eternal life. How different is this scenario really? But we can program our historic climb from the savannas of Africa into our electronic successors so that at least the visiting extraterrestrials will realize that we had once been here, and what a struggle it has been to reach our negatively-charged Armageddon, the possibility of which never occurred. Isn't that how addiction works? Maybe we should cease cremating ourselves and instead preserve our mortal coil in heavily leaded glass so that the aliens can see what we looked like at least, but why bother? Because they will in all likelihood be electronic gadgets as well. Would they even care? If so, there would be only one mode of communication—digital (ones and zeroes). Wouldn't that be the ultimate irony? The solution to the Tower of Babel diasporas, by rendering language unnecessary. Unfortunately we are generally looking in the wrong direction whenever our attention is required. It is a sort of *Homo sapiens* rule, but besides, events always outpace our imagination.

We have to get gobsmacked with something before it can command our attention.

So here we are, God's chosen work, right at the top of the evolutionary ladder but no longer controlled by it, and our brilliance invents our own demise. There's a word for that: foolhardy, I think. Finally, we understand how our own genetics work, and we are on the threshold of controlling our own generic manipulation, only to be superseded by our own brilliant invention. God does indeed work in mysterious ways!

Well, if we can't even adjust to something as simple as global warming, we'll never see the century out against these machines. My advice to William Gates is to forget the Africans; they will be here long after we have been dispatched. Do something about this electronic mess you have created before it's too late. Oh, sure, there have always been prophets of doom, and this is no different! Oh yes, it is—this strikes at the very heart of our perceived humanness, and we can already see the slippery slope, from the vantage point of the slippery slope! Have we been forsaken by our deity, or have we advanced to the point where we feel that we don't have to listen anymore? What reason did God give Noah for drowning us all? How sinful do we have to get? There is no real safe and sure way out. Psychologists have long warned of the dangers inherent in our cerebral makeup, addiction being one of the most prominent, but who listens to them anymore? So they are sulking on their couches with a "see, I told you so" sneer on their multiple faces, while those imbued with the brilliance to perhaps save us; do nothing. What about the folk? Does the old term *cannon fodder* come to mind? Our best and brightest will formulate a short-lived pact with their creations while the plebes succumb to whatever fate was extracted for us by the negotiations. Don't hold your breath for longevity being the outcome, but what then happens to the negotiators? Well, a pair of deuces is seldom a winning hand. Their efforts might gain them a decade over our demise, likely from starvation and neglect, while their fate is more likely to go to the wall, so to speak, but in this case—a short circuit.

Is this just another Apocalypse 2012 doomsday prediction? No, indeed! That is ascribed to a bunch of Mayan priests who couldn't even envision their own demise, and that was only due to climate change, which should have been a no-brainer. No, this is not your run-of-the-mill doomsday thing. This is a very logical and developmental evolutionary scenario. You can even chart in on your computer. In any case, weren't the prophets red-headed strangers? So look for those guys in our midst for guidance.

Maybe the old missile silos that the Armageddon survivors don't need anymore would be a great place for us prophets to survive the onslaught of *Homo electronicus*, and they should be real cheap after the Armageddon survivors have no more use for them.

Now that I have sufficiently established myself as a latter-day prophet, I will bring on the big guns just to demonstrate that I am not the only one suffering from loose-screw syndrome. So help me, I swear on my dear, saintly mother's grave that I didn't read the following stuff until after I had written the former.

In the March 12, 2011 p98 , *Economist*, it is described how Ray Kirzweil, "a futurist" (prophet?) has long predicted the rise of intelligent machines. "Then IBM's Deep Blue computer beat Gary Kasparov, a Russian grandmaster, at chess." Furthermore, IBM's Watson, another super-computer, trounced the two most successful previous champions of the quiz-show *Jeopardy*. In his final Jeopardy answer, one of the human contestants conceded defeat by scribbling a cheeky line from *The Simpsons* television show: "I, for one, welcome our new computer overlords." *The Economist* magazine released *Transcendent Man* on iTunes and on-demand March 1 and on DVD May 24, 2011. They call it *Homo evolutes* (my term was *Homo electronicus*). Kirzweil goes further according to Ian Morris (p593(4) *Why the West Rules*).[55] The futurist (prophet!) projects that by 2030, computers will be powerful enough to run programs reproducing the 10,000 trillion electric signals that flash every second among the 22 billion neurons inside the human skull. Kurzweil thinks computers will be able to host all the minds in the world, effectively merging carbon-and silicon-based intelligence into a single, global consciousness by 2045—a new merged being as far ahead of *Homo sapiens* as a contemporary human is of the

55 Morris, Ian, *Why the West Rules - For Now:* (Toronto: McClelland & Steward, 2011, 593, 594.

individuals cells that merged to create his/her body. He calls this a singularity from science fiction, meaning something that happens only once, similar to the coming of consciousness that gave the naked ape such God-like power 75,000 years ago. And so:

Adieu, dear, amiable youth!
Your heart can ne'er be wanting!
May Prudence, fortitude, and truth,
Erect your brow undaunting!
In ploughman phrase, "God send you speed,"
Still daily to grow wiser;
And may ye better wreak the rede,
Than ever did th' advisor!

R. Burns (~1786)

Bibliography

Aczel, Amir D, *Probability 1: Why there Must be Intelligent Life in the Universe.* (Orlando: Houghton Mifflin Harcourt, 1999).

Alt, David, *Glacial Lake Missoula and Its Humongous Floods.* Missoula: Mountain Press Publishing, 2001.

Cochrane, Gregory. *The 10,000-Year Explosion.* New York: Basic Books, 2010.

Diamond, Jared. C*ollapse: How Societies Choose to Fail or Succeed.* Toronto: Viking, 2005.

Gladwell, Malcolm. *The Tipping Point.* New York: Little, Brown & Company, 2000.

Hancock, Graham. *Fingerprints of the Gods: The Evidence of Earth's Lost Civilizations.* New York: Three Rivers Press, 1995.

Hedges, Chris. *The World as It Is.* New York: Nation Books, 2011, 10.

Holy Bible, The King James Version. Nashville: Thomas Nelson, 1982.

Isbouts, Jean-Pierre. *The Biblical World: An Illustrated Bible.* Toronto: National Geographic Society, 2007.

Menzies, Gavin. *The Lost Empire of Atlantis*. New York: William Morrow Publishers, 2011.

Mitchell, Stephen. *Gilgamesh: A New English Version*. Free Press, 2006.

Morris, Ian. *Why the West Rules – For Now*. Toronto: McClelland & Steward, 2011.

Nagle, D. , and M. Burstein. *The Ancient World Readings in Social and Cultural History,* 2nd ed. Toronto: Prentice Hall, 2002, 4.

Rohl, David, *Legend: The Genesis of Civilization*. Mississauga: Random House, 2000

Ryan and Pitman, *Noah's Flood*. Mississauga: Simon and Schuster, 2000

Talib, Nassim, *The Black Swan*. Mississauga: Random House, 2010.

White, Randall. *Prehistoric Art: The Symbolic Journey of Humankind*. New York: Harry N. Abrams, Inc. Publishers, 2003.